I know what Michael Framberger presents in this book can work because I've seen it work for him. He combines fresh new insights with proven quick tips that can be used in both your business and personal life. Whether you're looking for a motivational tool, a resource guide, or a wake-up call, this book delivers.

– Alan Katz, RHU, past president, National Association of Health Underwriters

I have been fortunate to meet thousands of motivators in my lifetime. But Michael is unique in that he not only teaches the way, he lives it as well. I have never met a more disciplined, driven man. His dreams have become a reality. And now he shares his secrets so yours can too!

– James Lloyd, author of *I'm on Fire, Watch Me Burn*

GET HAPPY GET HEALTHY BE WEALTHY

It's your choice

MICHAEL FRAMBERGER

HHW Press
San Luis Obispo, California

Get Happy, Get Healthy, Be Wealthy

Published by HHW Press
a division of Michael G. Framberger Seminars, Inc.
P.O. Box 14942 ■ San Luis Obispo, CA 93406
(800) 616-6210
www.gethappy-gethealthy-bewealthy.com

Printed in USA
Book design Sara Patton

ISBN: 0-9758720-0-1

Contents

To my wonderful wife and best friend, Connie, who has put up with all of my intensity for the last 30 years, especially the past two years as I wrote this book and started a whole new business while still working full-time. Thank you and I love you.

To my parents, George and Jane Framberger, 90 and 85, who throughout my life have been the consummate examples of happiness, health, and the true meaning of wealth.

Foreword

When I set out to write this book, my goal was to provide the reader with a "toolbox," a compendium of tools, tips, and resources of useful information that they could use to make serious and significant improvements in their lives. As David Allen stated in his endorsement of the book, there is a huge gap in what people know they should do and actually implementing it and getting it done.

My goal was to develop a simple yet effective system that would allow people to identify those areas of their lives where they felt they needed significant improvement or change; help them develop realistic, long-term, achievable goals and sustainable results; and provide them with the tools necessary to make that vision a reality.

Remember, it is all about choice. You make hundreds of choices every day and I want to help you make the most valuable choices. The design used throughout this book and the website at www.gethappy-gethealthy-bewealthy.com is intended to be like a keyhole to allow you to peek through and see your vision, then attend one of my seminars, so you can find the key to unlock your goals, your vision, and your potential.

The book is one component of an entire system that includes an interactive website, e-zine, newspaper column, and live seminars. Throughout the book, you will find numerous tips, book references, and web resources, all designed to provide you with the information and inspiration necessary to help you make the best choices to achieve your vision.

Over the past few years, I have gone through a tremendous amount of personal transformation in my own life. I have rebuilt my career, I have rebuilt my relationships, and, most recently, I have *completely* rebuilt my body. There are numerous examples of the transformations in this book and I believe that much of it is transferable. But the book is not about me; it is about *you*. I want to help you find ways to be able to choose those things in your life that will result in significantly greater satisfaction and self-actualization. You have to make the right choices. You can continue the way you are or you can choose to make the changes in your life that are necessary to achieve the results that you require. It is your choice.

This is not a one-time, read-through book. I would encourage you to review it frequently. My guess is that, as you explore more areas of change and inspiration in your life, things that may not have been meaningful to you in the first reading may come back and offer a great deal of value the second time around. The website is constantly being updated with new information that will also keep you abreast of current developments and provide a constant reminder of your choices and commitments. Please check it frequently and, if you have not already done so, sign up for the free e-zine.

If you only read this book, we may never actually meet, but it is my desire to develop as much of a relationship with you as possible through the other forms of the system. I would highly encourage you to attend one of the live seminars. It may very well be life-changing for you. Please remember that it comes with a no-questions-asked, money-back guarantee. If you follow the system and do not see significant improvement in the area you are seeking to change, I will gladly give you your money back.

Finally, if you find this information useful, I would be honored if you would share that thought and pass it on to a colleague or friend. My overall goal is to touch as many lives as I can. A referral from you may help someone you care about attain a level of happiness, health, and wealth that they did not think was possible.

Part 1

THE CHOICE

There are no limits to what you can be, have, or do,
except the ones you place on yourself.

– Brian Tracy

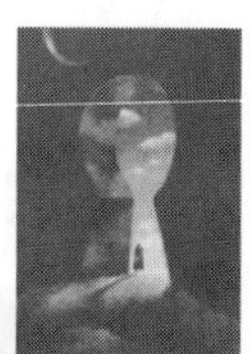

CHAPTER 1

It's All About Choice

Whether you think you can or you can't, you're probably right.

– Henry Ford

Every day, we are bombarded with invaluable information about how we can improve our lives. Yet remarkably few people are truly living lives of fulfillment and purpose.

All of us want to live the best life possible. And more often than not, we have a pretty good idea of how we could improve things. But the gap between *knowing what to do* and *actually doing it* keeps getting wider.

If you're like most people, you can quickly think of five things, right now, that you could do to improve your happiness, your health, or your wealth—that you are *not* doing!

So, why is that?

What are you waiting for? What would it take for you to choose to do the things you know will improve your life? You have everything to gain and nothing to lose.

But let me give you a tip: You can't get there by wanting it. You won't change a thing if all you do is sit around and dream: "I wish my marriage were happier . . . I wish I could lose 10 pounds and lower my cholesterol . . . I wish I had enough money so that I could not only provide for my own retirement, but also create multiple generations of wealth."

QUICK TIP
95% of your results come from 5% of your actions.

You've got to take action. And, before that, you've got to choose the best action to take. Hands down, the number one reason people fail to make changes in their lives is the lack of clearly set goals. There's no point trying to get anywhere, if you don't know exactly where you're going. As Zig Ziglar famously says, "How can you possibly hit a target you can't even see?"

There are those who work all day, those who dream all day, and those who spend an hour dreaming before setting to work to fulfill those dreams. Go into the third category because there's virtually no competition.

– Steven J. Ross

So, the choice is up to you. Are you going to continue doing what you're doing and hope that something will change for the better in your life? Or are you really going to take responsibility for your life and claim your power to change everything you want to change?

Because I've got news for you. If you're like most people and you keep things going the way they are, the odds are not good that you'll be happy or healthy or wealthy. In fact, it's nearly inevitable that you won't be. If you let yourself fall into the general mass of people who dream their way through life, never taking action and just hoping for the best, the statistics are pretty clear. Let your life drift into the status quo and here's exactly what you can expect . . .

ENDORPHIN INJECTION
It's always sunny above the clouds! Cheer up with a FREE monthly newsletter by Amanda Gore at www.amandagore.com.

HAPPINESS: WHAT'S THE STATUS QUO?

When it comes to happiness, things are pretty bleak. For all of the amenities in our modern lives, the happiness of the average person is plummeting. One of the leading causes of this unhappiness is said to be stress.

Studies have shown that as many as 70% of all physician office visits are stress-related. A significant number of those patients have moved beyond feeling stressed out and unhappy into chronic depression.

As many as one in five adults in America suffers from depression. Anti-depressant drugs are being prescribed for our children at an alarming rate. And the trend continues through high school and college. Almost one in ten college students reports that they considered suicide the year before. Depression costs the American economy $43.7 billion a year.

This lack of happiness inevitably shows up in our homes. The United States has one of the highest divorce rates in the world. As many as 50% of all marriages end up in divorce.

HEALTH: WHAT'S THE STATUS QUO?

When it comes to health, there is some truly exciting news. Physicians and scientists around the world are making great strides in uncovering the genetic roots of disease and treating the symptoms. Yet the diseases that are still killing us are those that are affected by our own habits and behaviors.

LEARN & LIVE QUIZ
Take a free quiz with potentially lifesaving information by the American Heart Association at www.americanheart.org.

Being challenged in life is inevitable; being defeated is optional.

– Roger Crawford

Heart disease is the number one killer in America. Although it used to be found more often in men, it is now the most common cause of death in women. One-third of all women will develop cardiovascular problems by the age of 45. More women will die from heart disease this year than from the next seven causes of death combined, yet it is one of the easiest diseases to prevent.

At least two-thirds of all cancer deaths can be prevented by lifestyle changes. The information is readily available. Yet people keep dying. They know what to do. Maybe they even tell themselves they *want* to do it. But they don't make the change. They drift.

Smoking, another completely voluntary action, is considered to be the greatest health risk of all. Obesity and weight problems are next. Type II diabetes, due primarily to weight gain, is one of the fastest growing diseases in America.

> **WEB REFERENCE**
> **For facts & figures about cancer, positive lifestyle changes, and much more, check out www.cancer.org.**

The odds of dying from heart disease, cancer, obesity, and diabetes can be decreased—or at least minimized—by simple lifestyle changes that everyone knows, or should know. But people who drift along in life without making a powerful choice to take charge of their future and change their habits are in serious danger from these diseases.

In some cases, the difference between life and death can come down to taking a brisk walk every day or making a change in diet. And still, people don't do it. *If they won't take action to save their own lives, when will they take action?*

> *I know of no more encouraging fact than the unquestionable ability of man to elevate his life by conscious endeavor.*
>
> – Henry David Thoreau

WEALTH: WHAT'S THE STATUS QUO?

When it comes to wealth, things are not much better. Everybody knows that credit card debt, bankruptcy, negative net worth, and a lack of retirement savings will have a dramatic impact on their lives in the future. But again, *knowing what to do* and *actually doing it* are miles apart.

Although the United States is one of the wealthiest countries on earth, we are buried in debt. The average American family has accumulated less than $10,000 in retirement savings and will not be able to afford to retire. More than half of all employees live from paycheck to paycheck and are one step away from financial disaster.

Consumer debt is the highest in our history and increasingly results in bankruptcy. When the baby boomer generation moves into retirement, the results of this lack of planning and preparation may well be disastrous.

The bottom line is this: You can't afford to let things drift and hope for the best. You have to get involved. As the old Latin proverb says, *"If the wind won't serve, put your back into the oars!"*

No one is going to do this for you. It's up to you. You are the only person who can ensure that you'll be happy, healthy, and wealthy for the rest of your life. If you genuinely want those things, you've got to make a choice to get them. Only *you* have the power to guarantee that change. Only *you* have the power to take control of your life. It's all about choice.

WILL YOU BE A SELF-MADE MILLIONAIRE?

Jerry L. Clark became a self-made millionaire in his twenties. From a very young age, he knew exactly what he wanted and he went after it. Maybe he got there sooner than you did. But if you really want it, you can make the same choice.

In fact, if you choose to be a millionaire now, you've got an advantage that Jerry Clark didn't have: You have the benefit of the lessons he's learned! They will help you hone in on your goal, maintain your focus, and get there much more quickly.

START WITH FIVE BASICS

1. Eliminate debt
2. Watch your spending
3. Tighten your budget
4. Save some money
5. Give some money away

For more tips from Chris Widener, visit www.yoursuccessstore.com.

All around the world, Clark shares the principles of his success in his bestselling programs, such as High Achievement Network Marketing and Creating Magic. When he says these three tips can enhance your performance, he knows what he's talking about!

1. **Clarity of outcome**

   Knowing in advance exactly what *outcome* you want to achieve creates future pull. It's like climbing a rope to the top of a cliff. By fastening the rope securely to your destination, you create a solid anchor that helps you make it to the top.

2. **Consolidation of power**

   You've only got so much energy and so many hours in a day. You've got to *focus* to consolidate your power. Clark talks about the familiar 80/20 rule. You're going to get 80% of your results from 20% of your activities. So don't spread yourself evenly among all the things you have to do. Figure out which things make up your 20%, then focus on that 20%. Consolidate your power on things with the highest payoff. It only makes sense.

3. **Commitment to discipline**

   Once you lock on securely to your outcome and focus on your 20%, it's time to *execute* your plan. Consistency is the key. As Clark points out, "Every day, in every way, you're either performing simple disciplines or simple errors in judgment."[1]

Put these three steps to work in your life. Your performance will soar!

---

[1] Clark, Jerry L. "Three Steps to Enhancing Your Personal Performance." Newsletter (1999), www.yoursuccessstore.com.

MAKING CHOICES THAT STICK

As a professional speaker, whenever I ask audiences if they want to get happy, get healthy, and be wealthy, what do you think they say? They say yes! What else would they say? I could walk up to strangers on the street—on any street around the world—and if I asked the same questions, I'd get the same reply. Do human beings want happiness, health, and wealth? Of course they do. Are they willing to make a choice to be get happy, get healthy, and be wealthy? Absolutely.

Then why do so few people have any one of those things as a dependable feature of their lives? What goes wrong?

People don't take action. In many cases, they don't take action because they don't have a plan and they haven't created the action steps that make a plan work. I'll say a lot more about this in Part 2. For now, let me just explain that the difference between those who fail and those who succeed is *consistent* action.

1. **Choose your goal.**

   "I want to lose 10 pounds before the holidays."

2. **Educate yourself.**

   You need to find out what's going to be involved in reaching your goal. You can't make an intelligent, well-informed plan if you haven't done your homework.

3. **Break your goal down into action steps.**

   Make a list of *exactly* what steps you'll take to turn your knowledge into action.

4. **Follow those action steps consistently.**

   This is key. If you only follow your long-term plan for a week, you can't get there from here. Step-by-step, day-after-day consistent action is what it takes.

Success is pretty straightforward: Think about what you want, find out how to get it, then do whatever it takes until you reach your goal.

It's just that easy. But here's the catch.

Things are going to get in your way. Most of them are you. Sure, now and then life will throw you a curve ball. Unexpected events will come into your life to slow you down, delay your plans, or even change your goals. More often than that, however, you'll have to contend with what goes on in your head.

What stops you from going to the gym every day? Has a tree been hit by lightning and fallen in front of your door, so you can't get out? Has your car been stolen in the night? Did the dog eat your gym shoes? Not likely. What stops you on the days you don't go is your own negative self-talk that says, "I don't feel like going to the gym today . . ."

What makes you buy a big-screen TV as soon as you get paid, instead of investing that money for your retirement? What makes you avoid talking to your partner about things, instead of putting in the time to build a happy relationship? What makes you grab a burger for lunch, instead of eating the salad you brought from home? The odds of someone forcing you to do any of these things are very low. Nine times out of ten, it's you. You go for the quick fix, the thing that makes you feel good *right now*—instead of holding out for the things that will make you feel better in the long run and add real quality to your life.

TOP 10 SELF-DEFEATING MENTAL HABITS

If you're like most people, the minute you start to take charge of your own life, you'll stumble across certain patterns that have made your life the way it is today. It can be a little embarrassing to recognize the ways you're contributing to your own problems.

But take heart. All of us have learned self-defeating patterns. And we can all overcome them. The first step is recognizing them. The second step is choosing to change them. It's entirely up to you.

Here are the top 10 self-defeating mental habits and the actions that go with them, according to Dr. Jeffrey Young, Ph.D., founder of the Cognitive Therapy Center of New York.[2]

TOP 10 SELF-DEFEATING MENTAL HABITS

Habit 1:	Abandonment
Action:	Clinging to relationships
Habit 2:	Deprivation
Action:	Overdoing it — spending more, eating more, working more, etc.
Habit 3:	Subjugation
Action:	Passive aggression
Habit 4:	Mistrust
Action:	Constantly offended by perceived slights
Habit 5:	Unlovability
Action:	Shyness out of fear of rejection
Habit 6:	Social exclusion
Action:	Anxiety in social groups
Habit 7:	Vulnerability
Action:	Worry leading to overpreparation and excessive caution
Habit 8:	Failure
Action:	Constant self-doubt, even feeling success is undeserved
Habit 9:	Perfectionism
Action:	Focus on what is wrong rather than what is right
Habit 10:	Entitlement
Action:	Selfishness and irritation with limits

[2] Bennett-Goleman, Tara. "Break Free," *Bottom Line, Personal* (Oct. 1, 2001).

TRANSFORM BAD HABITS INTO GOOD HABITS

What are your worst habits? Eating junk food? Bad time management? Negative thoughts? Taking your loved ones for granted? Procrastinating about your financial future?

James Claiborn, Ph.D., suggests several steps that can turn bad habits into good habits. Try these steps on one of your habits. If it works, make a list of five habits you want to change. Then eliminate them, one by one. There's no need to continue to do the lax and sloppy things you don't admire in yourself. You're in charge. Make the change!

1. Habit awareness

Spend the first week like a research scientist, observing yourself in action. When do you indulge in this habit? How often? Does something provoke it? Is it linked to a certain time of day? And, here's an important one: What are you *thinking* when you do it?

2. Change your thoughts

Most people don't notice what they're thinking when they're engaged in a bad habit. It's become too automatic. So *noticing* is a powerful key to undoing it. By noticing, you've already changed something!

Dr. Claiborn describes some common thoughts and suggestions for how to counteract these thoughts.
Try a few of these, then create your own.

You can begin to change your thoughts *today*—*right now!* Why wait?

3. Self-pitying thoughts

These are "Poor me, I've had a rough day . . ." thoughts. They seem like sympathy for yourself, but they actually make you feel worse—and *much* more inclined to indulge in a bad habit. What starts out as sympathy ends up as, "So I'll just have this giant slice of chocolate cake!" You don't need it. Self-pity saps your strength and makes you underestimate yourself. The best counteractive thought for self-pity: "But it's no big deal. I'm strong. I can take it."

4. Punishing thoughts

These thoughts are deliberately demoralizing. They focus their attack on *who you are.* Give them up. The second you hear yourself thinking, "I'm not good enough," "I'm a failure," or any other thought that sounds like an insult, *stop it!* You don't have to take that kind of thing from anyone — especially yourself! Whatever the thought is, counter it. Put your whole heart into it. Imagine yourself now, as an adult, standing down a schoolyard bully. This kid is so obvious. He feels bad about himself, so he's insulting you. Just let him have it, by saying: "I *am* good enough!" or "I *don't* suck at this!"

You are searching for the magic key that will unlock the door to the source of power, and yet you have the key in your own hands and you may use it the moment you learn to control your thoughts.

– Napoleon Hill

5. Defeating thoughts

These thoughts are drama queens. You forget your wife's birthday and your thoughts leap to this conclusion: "You're a terrible husband!" Not only do your thoughts exaggerate the evidence against you, but they wallow in it. There's something strangely tempting about being a hopeless case, isn't there? Go ahead. Admit it. If you're a hopelessly terrible husband, it takes the pressure off. You don't have to try and risk making an embarrassing mistake again, you're hopeless! Whew! Don't play yourself like this. It's cheap. You're better than that.

If taking vitamins doesn't keep you healthy, try more laughter!

– Nicolas-Sebastian Chamfort

6. Develop a competing habit

This suggestion is gold. Think about it. If you're busy doing something that's incompatible with your bad habit, you *can't* engage in the bad habit. You're busy. Dr. Claiborn gives the example of the bad habit of cutting people off by jumping in with your opinion. As soon as the urge comes up, count to 10. Not only will you slow your reaction but, in that time, the urge will diminish a bit too. Just enough time for you to remind yourself that this is a bad habit you're going to break. It lets you take charge again.

7. Build good habits

Good habits are the best counter-response there is. Keep it simple. Make it easy to engage in the new habit. Remember, your bad habit has had a lot longer to feel comfortable. The new habit is likely to feel a little weird and unnatural to you at first. That's normal. So cut yourself some slack. Make it as convenient for yourself as possible. If you've decided to start saving 10% of your income every week, make it simple. Don't give yourself the chance to spend that money. Don't rely on yourself to remember. Have it automatically taken from your account at regular intervals.

YOU CAN CHANGE YOUR SLEEP HABITS!
Not enough time in your week? Set your alarm clock 30 minutes earlier. In four or five days, your body will adjust and you will gain almost four hours a week! (If that's too severe, start with 10 minutes.)

8. Evaluate lapses

Because you've nailed your defeating and punishing thoughts, you're definitely not going to be indulging in blame and self-pity when a lapse comes along. You'll remember that nobody's perfect and it's far better to reach a series of nearly perfect goals than a miraculously perfect one. Any lapse is a great source of information. Notice what triggered it. Learn from your mistakes and you'll be stronger for every one you make!

We are continually faced with great opportunities
brilliantly disguised as insoluble problems.

– Lee Iacocca

PERFECTIONISM? GET OVER IT!

No one would argue that any of us are perfect. Yet a lot of us live as if we won't settle for anything less. We expect too much of others and we expect too much of ourselves.

Perfectionism is counterproductive. An inspiring vision can make us achieve more and reach higher, but perfectionism isn't focused on inspiration. It's focused on finding fault. It can ruin your relationships, stifle your creativity, and paralyze your success.

Veronique Vienne, author of *The Art of Imperfection: Simple Ways to Make Peace with Yourself*, offers five tips for getting over the drive for perfection. Put these tips into effect and you will free yourself from that merciless tyrant, perfectionism:

1. Plan to be imperfect.

Remember those days when you said yourself, "I might as well blow off the diet today, because I ate that candy bar"? No, that's perfectionism talking. You might as well stay on the diet. Try your best, but don't let perfectionism trick you into bailing out because you make a mistake.

2. Build in a false start.

Allow yourself to ease into things. If your goal is to work out at the gym for 30 minutes, three days a week, ease into it. It's hard to build a new habit. Start by getting yourself to the gym three days a week. Whether your workout is 30 minutes or not, it will get your blood pumping and give you a little taste of your goal. Then next week, you'll feel so much better that it'll be a lot easier to go! If you ignore the voice of perfectionism, you'll see the value of a "false start."

3. Negotiate a truce with yourself.

Perfectionism is closely aligned with pride. We all want to believe we're the best. Settling for less just doesn't give us the same heady rush of pride as doing something perfectly—in fact, better than anybody else!—every time. But get a grip. You're *not* going to do it perfectly every time. So you're better off to cut a deal with yourself to accept a little less than perfection for the sake of actually reaching your goals!

DO ONE THING DIFFERENTLY
"There *is* a way out. Figure out what you're doing . . . and do something *different!*" Bill O'Hanlon proves it works in *Do One Thing Different: 10 Simple Ways to Change Your Life.*

4. Stop looking at others.

The people who spend the most time telling everyone else about what they're going to do are *not* the ones who are busy doing it. Making big plans and letting everyone know how incredible it's going to be is a moment in the sun for perfectionism. Because talk is cheap. It all turns out perfectly when you talk about it. But you're wasting your time and using up the energy you need to reach your goals—not perfectly, but far better than you ever will by talking about them!

5. Value the process.

What's going to happen when you reach your biggest goal? Will you rest on your laurels, like a high school quarterback who won the big game back in the day? No. You'll set another big goal and reach it. Remembering this can go a long way to unshackling you from the chains of perfectionism. Yes, this goal is important. But you can stand a little imperfection, you can afford a few mistakes—because this isn't the *only* thing you'll ever be doing in your life. It's one success in a long series of successes that we like to call Your Life. So lighten up.

Out of clutter, find simplicity.
From discord, find harmony.
In the middle of difficulty lives opportunity.

– Albert Einstein

People waste a lot of energy on perfectionism, when they could be logging one nearly perfect success after another. Don't fall for it!

SUCCESS BREEDS SUCCESS

Your goals are just a wish list until you put them into action. In this book, I'll talk about choosing your goals, educating yourself, and creating action steps to reach your goals. Even with all of that, however, you need a mindset that will allow you to follow through consistently.

Athletes call it "mental toughness." It's the thing that makes a triathlete keep running when every muscle in his body is telling him to quit. Having raced in triathlons for over 20 years, I speak from experience. It takes mental toughness to push yourself to the limit in a competitive contest like that. That toughness is strengthened every day you train.

WHAT IS YOUR MENTAL TOUGHNESS QUOTIENT?

The Psychological Research Foundation singles out these five characteristics as evidence of mental toughness:

1. **Bounce back:** The ability to learn quickly from your mistakes and put your failures behind you.
2. **Pressure tolerance:** The ability to stay calm—or even thrive—under pressure.
3. **Concentration:** The ability to focus on your goals and put other things out of your mind.
4. **Confidence:** The ability to retain your confidence, regardless of setbacks.
5. **Motivation:** The ability to drive yourself to reach your goals.

The measure of these qualities is your mental toughness quotient. Take this free test online and find out just how tough you are! www.testsonthenet.com/mental-toughness/test-report-totnv2.htm.

Every time you take the action steps that bring you closer to your goals, you get stronger. Every time you move past the self-talk that says, "You're going to fail!" or "This is a bad idea!" or "I don't feel like it right now . . ." it gets easier to move past that talk the next time and do the things you've chosen to do. Success breeds success.

No matter how many times you've said you were going to change and didn't do it, there's no reason why you can't succeed this time. What makes champions succeed, even when others are doubting them? According to Chris Townsend, who has worked with champion swimmers for over a decade, "They simply never, ever give up . . . I am not saying that champions never doubt themselves. All champions waver at times. But somehow they manage to come up with enough belief in themselves to ride through it, overcome it, and beat it."[3]

If you have mental toughness, it means you have the strength to reach your goals, no matter what. Even when "everyone else is counting you out, you're counting yourself in!"[4]

No matter how many times you've said you wanted to be happier or healthier or wealthier, this is the time to make it happen. There's no doubt that you can do it. Make your choice and follow through. It's as easy (and as hard) as that.

> *Early in my career, many "cycling experts" typecast me as a one-day racer. They said I would never win a major multi-day race like the Tour de France. My victory supports the belief that anything is possible if you are willing to stick to your dream and keep trying.*
>
> – Lance Armstrong, six-time winner of the Tour de France

[3, 4] Townsend, Chris. "Mental Toughness." (August 9, 2004) swimming.about.com.

CHAPTER 2
Perception

Your outer world is a reflection of your inner world.
If you change your thinking, you change your life.

– Brian Tracy

Professional speaker and author of *New Sales Speak*, Terri Sjodin, asks people: "How do you peel a banana?" If you're like most adults, you've probably peeled hundreds—if not thousands—of bananas over your lifetime. How do you do it? You most likely peel it by grabbing hold of the stem, wrenching it loose from the peel on one side, then pulling it down. Since the stem is often tough and unyielding, you may have gotten into the habit of cutting the stem off, so you can peel the skin down more easily.

If that's the way you do it, you're in good company. You're resourceful, well-educated, and certainly know how to do something as basic as peeling a banana.

But I've got news for you. If you peel a banana that way in Central America or any other banana-growing country, they'll have a good chuckle at your expense. Some of the adults will simply shake their heads and mutter, "Dumb gringo . . ." But the children will actually point and laugh. "Look! An adult who doesn't even know how to peel a banana!"

In banana country, even a child knows that the best way to peel a banana is to leave the stem alone! Turn the banana upside down and pinch the non-stem end. It will open right up and peel very easily. As any Central American child will tell you, the stem is meant to be a handle to hold onto while you peel your banana! (Dumb gringo!)

Makes you wonder what else in your life are you doing "wrong," doesn't it? If you talked to people who knew better, how many things in your life could be improved as easily?

Do not wish to be anything but what you are,
and try to be that perfectly.

– St. Francis de Sales

The information's out there. It's abundant. Sometimes the solution is as simple as asking a child. Finding the solutions is easy. The hard part, for some adults, is being willing to change.

This book is filled with solutions. By picking and choosing carefully, I have culled them from the some of the richest resources of information in the world. Many of them have changed my own life in ways I never thought possible! So I know what they can do. And I'm passionate about sharing them with you.

But I also know for a fact that information is not enough. My passion about passing these solutions on to you is not enough. You have to be willing to change. You have to be willing to take control of your life and make new choices.

SKIP THE BLAME!
We all progress by taking two steps forward and one step back. There's no doubt about it: You *will fail.* That's par for the course. The sooner you move past it, the sooner you'll succeed. Moving on puts the odds in your favor. Blame only slows you down. So *skip it!*

The choices won't always be comfortable at first. They're not necessarily going to feel right. I have to tell you, when I made a commitment to do 75 minutes of circuit training every other morning before work, it wasn't comfortable. On that first day, when the alarm went off at 4:30 A.M., a perfectly rational voice inside my head, said, "What? Are you nuts?!" But I got out of bed anyway and worked out. The second time, it was more of the same. The third time, I woke up stiff and sore, which made it even harder. Every morning, I reminded myself that I'd made my choice to get fit and this was going to work. Despite the discomfort, I just kept doing it anyway.

Being miserable is easy.
Being happy is tougher—and cooler!

– Thom Yorke

Major change is *usually* uncomfortable. Since the payoff doesn't necessarily come instantaneously, change takes a little more patience and faith than most of us would prefer. But if you can stick it out, the sky's the limit! The rewards for your hard work can be just about anything you set your mind on!

In a very short time, my circuit training began to pay off in ways that made it easier for me to hop out of bed *before* my alarm rang. Even before I started seeing incredible changes in my body, the workouts were giving me so much energy that I didn't *want* to give them up!

It can be that way for you—whether you're trying to get happy, get healthy, or be wealthy. You can completely change your life, if you're willing to change.

Let me ask you this: How did you respond to the banana story? Did you think, "Peeling from the bottom? That's too weird! It works just fine the way I've always done it"? Or did you think, "How great! I'm going to go find a banana and try that out"?

We live in a time of amazing knowledge and opportunity. Solutions abound. You have the power to change the things in your life that you always dreamed of changing. Are you open to exploring change? Are you willing to consider new ideas? Are you ready to make your choice, stand by it, and do whatever it takes to reach your goals?

Who are you? Do you have what it takes? Like the Gatorade commercial says, "Is it in you?"

HOW MUCH DO YOU KNOW ABOUT YOU?

If you don't know you, who does? Cheerfulness guru Amanda Gore offers these great tips for getting back in touch with yourself:

1. Have a conversation with your heart every day.
2. Slow down long enough to let your soul catch up.
3. Cultivate a sense of belonging in your life.
4. Find one thing to be grateful for, every morning and every night.
5. Celebrate the small things!

For an infusion of hope and inspiration, check out Amanda Gore's website at www.amandagore.com.

WHAT'S YOUR POINT OF VIEW?

Like most children, I was deathly afraid of the dark when I was young. Sure that all forms of unspeakable evil happened in the dark, I would sometimes lie in my bed frozen with fear while I waited for it to get light outside. More often than not, I fell asleep waiting.

As a teenager, my point of view changed. Young and full of vitality, I was enamored by the dark. When I could get away with it, I would sometimes stay out all night just to experience the mystery and intrigue of the darkness. The fear and uncertainty that had paralyzed me some nights as a little boy was hard to understand.

As a pragmatic, middle-aged man, I am ambivalent toward the dark. It's become the thing that happens in the evening, after daylight. The dark holds no mystery or fascination. It neither makes me pull the covers over my head nor yearn to crawl out the window to explore its mysteries. I remember those earlier points of view, but they are not my own anymore. I've changed.

When I grow elderly, it would not be uncommon for me to fear the dark once again. It will not be the fear of the unknown and its imaginary monsters that I knew as a young boy. The dark presents the elderly with real and apparent dangers due to their vulnerability and frailty. My earlier points of view will be moot in these new circumstances.

Over the course of my life, the dark will not have changed, but my perspective toward the dark will change again and again. From each new point of view, I will dismiss the others as irrelevant and meaningless to me, even though each of them had once been my own.

What in your life will change over time, as you change?

Age and experience change our perspective on many things. But knowledge can change our perspective as well. Like so many other things, our perspective is a matter of choice. The attitude we bring to our lives can make us see obstacles or opportunities.

If you truly want to change your life, a change in your attitude is a good place to start!

If you don't have a vision for the future,
then your future is destined to be a repeat of the past.

– A.R. Bernard

TURNING OBSTACLES INTO OPPORTUNITIES

In her book, *Choose the Happiness Habit*, Pam Golden makes it clear that we can choose to turn our obstacles into opportunities or choose to let them defeat us.

To illustrate this point, she gives the example of twin brothers from an alcoholic family.

> One brother grows up to be an alcoholic, living on the streets. The other brother becomes a successful businessman at the head of his own company.
>
> One day, a social worker, giving soup to the homeless, asks the one brother, "Why did you become an alcoholic?"

"My father was a drunk," he replies.

On the same day, a journalist who is profiling prominent businesspeople asks the other brother, "What is the secret of your success?"

"My father was a drunk," he replies.

What makes one brother choose failure and the other choose success? What makes one brother see a dead end, where the other sees a road to success? Which brother are you like?

BOOK REFERENCE

What makes some people happier than others? Studies show that people who had won the lottery were no happier than people who didn't. Even people who had been paralyzed in an accident were only slightly less happy than they were before. In his book, *Authentic Happiness,* Dr. Martin Seligman of the University of Pennsylvania shows how to increase your basic happiness quotient, so you'll be able to hang onto a sense of contentment and well-being, no matter what happens in your life.

ARE YOU LIVING THE PROBLEM OR LIVING THE SOLUTION?

I couldn't agree more with what Bob Proctor always says: "You're either living in the problem or you're living in the solution." Where do you put your attention? Even if it's not obvious to you, you can bet it's obvious to everyone around you.

People who live the problem attract problems. If you love to live the problem, don't worry: You'll never have a shortage. You'll start seeing problems everywhere. Before too long, even the solutions will start looking like problems!

Here's an example of the same guy in the same situation—living the problem or living the solution.

Living the problem

A guy who lives the problem is reading a book in his living room when the bulb in his reading light goes out. "Typical!" he mutters. He goes to the closet to get another bulb, only to discover that there are no light bulbs left in the closet.

Still muttering and feeling sorry for himself, he goes to buy another bulb. At the store, it's one problem after another. First, he can't find the light bulbs, because they've rearranged the store. Annoyed, he asks a clerk where the bulbs are, but the clerk is rude and not inclined to help.

When he does find the bulb on his own, the price isn't marked, so the cashier has to go look it up. Looking for an outlet for his frustration, he decides the cashier is an idiot. By the time he gets home, he's annoyed and stressed out. Life feels hard and unfair. It seems that even the simplest thing is a problem.

> **DON'T GET STUCK ON *WHY?!***
> Dr. Sylvia Boorstein says it's natural to ask "Why?!" or "Why *me*?!" when something goes wrong. But all too often, asking "Why?" only makes us feel more miserable. There's a better response. It puts you back in charge. Instead of asking "Why?" ask: "What do I *do* now?"

To make matters worse, by this time his cortisol levels are too high to settle into reading. He now has a physical need for stress relief. He could decide to meditate, work out, or take a long walk, but he'd have to change clothes for that and it seems like too much effort. He's so angry and keyed up that he's more likely to turn to less healthy choices—like smoking, drinking, overeating, or spending all night in front of the TV.

Living the solution

Now suppose this same guy turns his life around. Unhappy with his life, he attends a couple of workshops and reads some books. He soon recognizes that living the problem is making him miserable. With practice, he gradually learns how to live the solution instead.

Then, about a year later, he's reading a book like this one in his living room, when the bulb in his reading light goes out. "No problem," he says. "I'll replace the bulb." He goes to the closet but, of course, there are no bulbs left. So he drives to the store.

Turns out they've rearranged the store again and he can't find the bulbs. "No problem," he says. "I'll just ask someone." With a friendly smile, he approaches a clerk, who is glad to show him where the bulbs are. They laugh together about how often this store gets rearranged.

When he takes the bulb to the counter, the price isn't on it, but the cashier is kind enough to go look it up. Looking for a way to express his appreciation, he has a pleasant exchange with the cashier and leaves smiling. By the time he gets home, he feels happier. He notices he has an extra boost of energy. It's such a beautiful night, he decides to go for a walk. He'll have to change his clothes, of course, but that's no problem. Besides, it'll be good for his heart.

The secret of life is enjoying the passage of time.

– James Taylor

WHAT YOU REALLY NEED

Psychologist Abraham Maslow was famous for his creation of the Hierarchy of Needs.[5] He identified the five most basic needs we all need to satisfy. They occur in this order:

1. **Physiological**

   The need for the basic necessities of food, water, air, clothing, and shelter.

2. **Security**

   The need for safety, stability, and lack of pain or sickness.

3. **Affiliation**

   The need for affection, friendship, love, and belonging.

[5] http://web.utk.edu/~gwynne/maslow.HTM

4. **Esteem**

   The need for self-worth, respect, and recognition from others.

5. **Self-actualization**

   The need for fulfillment and reaching of personal potential.

One of Maslow's most interesting discoveries was that these are not just our most important needs. They are our most important needs *in order*. Each of the more basic needs must be met *before* we can go on to the other needs.

If you've ever had a toothache that was so intense it became the absolute focus of your attention, you'll know what Maslow meant. Fulfillment and self-esteem are great. Having friends who love you is essential. But if you have a blindingly painful toothache, it's all you can think about. Until you handle the need for lack of pain, you can't really spend much time on the more advanced needs on the hierarchy.

On the other hand, if your security was imperiled in another way, it would feel like an important priority too. Suppose, for example, that you are on your way to the dentist, when your car breaks down on the freeway. Your tooth is still killing you. But you need to secure your situation first. A physiological need—such as running out of oxygen —would also take precedence.

When you're making new choices in your life, Maslow's Hierarchy is an important tool. It provides an important guide to what you *really* need. You can see at a glance that even needs as important as love and respect take second place to lack of pain or sickness. No matter how happy you are in your relationships or how wealthy you become in other ways, your health is a prerequisite. A toothache is easily resolved. But high cholesterol, obesity, or heart disease are longer-term problems that literally put your life at risk.

As you begin to consider ways to improve your life in the chapters that follow, keep Maslow's Hierarchy in mind. It will help you remember to keep the most important needs secure, while you build an exciting new future.

Ask yourself, "Will it really matter five years from now?"

– Anonymous

QUIZ: WHO LOVES YOU, BABY?

In her monthly Endorphin Injection newsletter (September 2003), Amanda Gore points out that true satisfaction in life comes from love, not success, status, wealth, or power.

Answer these questions (inspired by that newsletter) to identify how much love you have in your life.

1. How much do you love yourself?

As the old saying goes, "You can't give someone else something that you don't have." What holds true for the loved ones in your life holds true for you as well. Treat yourself with kindness. Forgive your mistakes. Show that you care.

2. Do you treat others in a loving way?

Are you alert to their needs? Do you notice when they're feeling down? Are you available to share their joys and sorrows? Listening, soothing words, affection, kindness, touch, attention—these are only a few of the ways you can treat others with love every day.

3. Have you told others you love them?

Telling others you love them is important. There is no need to restrict yourself to one format or venue. Write a letter. Make a call. Send an e-mail. Tell them in person. A combination of all of these—and anything else you can think of—works wonders. The key is: Do it frequently!

4. Do you spend time with your loved ones?

All of us have such busy schedules that time has become more precious than money. In human relations, taking time with people we love has always been one of the best ways to show we care. It's nice to spend 30 minutes buying a gift, but even more memorable to spend 30 minutes holding someone's hand and telling them how much they mean to you.

For more tips on amplifying the love and joy in your life, go to www.amandagore.com.

If only I may grow firmer, simpler,
quieter, warmer.

– Dag Hammarskjold

QUIZ: PUTTING FIRST THINGS FIRST

According to career and relationships consultant Jessica Haynes, the eight items below are often listed as the key satisfactions in people's lives. Ironically, people don't always prioritize the things that are most satisfying to them. Do you?

Number the items below in order of their importance to you. Then ask yourself this: How much time do you spend on the ones you value most?

- ❑ A feeling of control in my life
- ❑ An important love relationship
- ❑ A satisfying job or career
- ❑ Good friends
- ❑ Time to relax
- ❑ Exercise
- ❑ A spiritual connection
- ❑ Hope

For more information on empowerment, productivity, and success, check out Jessica Haynes' website at www.aspirenow.com.

WHY NOT BE AN OPTIMIST?

When you make a mistake, do you tell yourself, "I'm an idiot!" or do you say to yourself, "That's odd . . . I must be off my game today"? Are you surprised when things go wrong or do you expect disaster? When you succeed, do you consider it a fluke or a natural outcome of your efforts?

How you see the world determines how you will react when things go right or wrong.

If you have a pessimistic attitude, you may actually be uncomfortable when things are going well. Good news will make you feel uneasy and suspicious, as if you're "waiting for the other shoe to drop." Without even realizing it, you may actually *prefer* for things to go badly, because that matches your beliefs about the world.

By contrast, if you have an optimistic attitude, you will be more likely to expect good news. Bad news will seem like the *exception* to the rule. You'll be eager to make things go well again, since you believe that to be the norm.

Dr. Martin Seligman explains that pessimists and optimists view events very differently. All of us tend to draw conclusions that support

BOOK REFERENCES

The ancient practice of meditation is known to increase creativity, strengthen the immune system, improve the ability to focus, and decrease blood pressure as well as cholesterol. Check out these two valuable books on the subject:

***Insight Meditation Kit: A Step-by-Step Course on How to Meditate* by Sharon Salzberg and Joseph Goldstein (Sounds True, 2001). This kit includes a workbook, study cards, and two CDs. It can be found at soundstrue.com — a rich website, filled with the latest resources on personal development.**

***Wherever You Go, There You Are: Mindfulness Meditation in Everyday Life* by Jon Kabat-Zinn (Hyperion, 1995).**

our points of view. Amazingly enough, the same event can seem good or bad—depending on your perspective.

As you read the examples below, ask yourself two things:

1. Are you more likely to take an optimistic or pessimistic point of view?
2. Since it's all in how you look at it, *Why not be an optimist?*

SITUATION: You win a game of squash.
A pessimist says: "The other player was having an off day."
An optimist says: "My game has really improved!"

SITUATION: You forget an appointment.
A pessimist says: "I'm getting old!"
An optimist says: "This is so unusual for me."

SITUATION: You go on a diet, but don't lose weight.
A pessimist says: "I'll never lose weight."
An optimist says: "I'll have to switch to a diet that works for me."

SITUATION: You have a wonderful marriage.
A pessimist says: "I'm lucky I found someone who'd have me."
An optimist says: "We both give this marriage our best."

SITUATION: You have a conflict with your coworkers.
A pessimist says: "People will stab you in the back if they have the chance!"
An optimist says: "They've been under a lot of stress lately."

SITUATION: You run for office and win.
A pessimist says: "I'm lucky."
An optimist says: "I'm the right person for this job."

Dr. Seligman offers several free self-tests to evaluate your levels of optimism, happiness, and a range of positive emotions on his website: www.authentichappiness.org. The results are confidential.

He that lives on hope will die fasting.

– Benjamin Franklin

LAY CLAIM TO YOUR LIFE!

When you're young, a lot of things are decided for you. Most likely, your parents decided where you grew up, what school you went to as a child, what clothes you wore, what time you went to bed, and a host of other things.

It isn't like that anymore.

Strangely enough, a lot of people don't seem to realize it! They get into the habit of having things decided for them when they're young and never take charge of their own lives. They never seem to notice how many different choices are available to them now. Years pass them by. Golden opportunities come and go. Yet they don't rise to the challenge of defining their lives on their own terms. They never really make an active choice about what they want to do.

You can live like that too, if you want to. It's easy. Here's how:

Do nothing.

Whatever happens—for better or worse—just shrug. Feel free to dream, if you'd like. As long as you never take action, dreaming will have little or no effect on your results. But that's OK. When your dreams don't come true, you can just shake your head and sigh, "It wasn't meant to be ..." and keep drifting to your heart's content.

QUICK TIP

When scientists want to prove the calming effects of music, they often turn to *Pachelbel's Canon in D Major*. Time and again, it's shown to lower blood pressure, heart rate, and anxiety. This is one soothing piece of music! If you don't own a copy, now's the time to buy one!

It's as if you're living in a boat on the ocean. Your boat has beautiful sails, but they're not unfurled. It has a perfectly good rudder, but you never use it. You prefer to let the sea take you where it will.

Perhaps you'll end up in a beautiful resort town with friendly people, plenty of fresh food, and a hospitable climate. Perhaps you'll end up on a deserted island with harsh winds and very little vegetation. No matter. You'll adapt. "What will be, will be" is your motto. You'll find a way to be content with whatever comes along.

It's always good to make the best of things. But why make the best of a deserted island, when you could be making the best of a beautiful resort town?

Sometimes the only difference is *action*. If you've been drifting through your life, you can choose to *stop drifting* right now. It's never too late. Take the helm! Hoist the sails! Lay claim to your own life today!

BOOK REFERENCE

All of us tend to make up worst-case scenarios in our heads. Psychiatrist Gregg D. Jacobs of Harvard Medical School teaches cognitive restructuring (CR) to help turn *off* the negative thoughts that undermine our well-being. Learn more about it in his fascinating book, *The Ancestral Mind: Reclaim the Power.*

With knowledge comes opportunity.
With perseverance comes success.

– J.C. Johnstone

Part 2

GET HAPPY

People are about as happy as they make up their minds to be.

– Abraham Lincoln

CHAPTER 3

Choosing Happiness

The only true happiness comes from squandering ourselves for a purpose.

– John Mason Brown

Are you happy? *How* happy? Are you bubbling over with happiness or quietly content? Do you walk through your day with an easy smile that says, "My life is good"? Or are you so caught up in rushing from one activity to the next that you don't have time to notice whether things are good or not?

Tell yourself the truth: *Do you wish you were happier?*

You can be.

I'm happy and I can show you how. In order to "get happy," you have to focus on happiness—literally immerse yourself in it. In this chapter and those that follow, you will find a variety of tools—tips, references, books, websites, quizzes, and exercises—that will help you reach your goal. But you'll have to make use of those resources for yourself. It is up to you to choose to implement those tools and make sure that you get happy.

Fleeting happiness is as fickle and changeable as the weather. A smile from a child or a kiss from a lover can suffuse you with momentary joy. Lasting happiness isn't something that comes over you in a flash. It's something you choose. Whether you live a happy life or not is entirely up to you. It always has been.

The joy of life consists in the exercise of one's energies, continual growth, constant change, the enjoyment of every new experience. The eternal mistake of mankind is to set up an unattainable ideal.

– Aleister Crowley

ELIMINATING THE CULPRITS

What gets in your way? What are the things that make you say, "fine" instead of "great!" when someone asks you how you are? What are the culprits that interfere with your happiness? And how are you going to get rid of them?

Take a moment to write down the first five things that come to mind when you say, "Why am I unhappy?"

1. ______________________________
2. ______________________________
3. ______________________________
4. ______________________________
5. ______________________________

Now ask yourself, "What can I do about it?" This one may take a little more thought. When you've come up with a potential solution, write your answer below, next to the corresponding number:

1. ______________________________
2. ______________________________
3. ______________________________
4. ______________________________
5. ______________________________

OVERCOMING DEPRESSION

Everyone wants to feel happier, and in recent years a boom market has risen up in "happiness fixes." Some of them work better than others, and some work better for some people than for others.

According to *Prevention* magazine (October 2002), millions of Americans say that they feel less depressed—but not great—when they try supplements, anti-depressants, talk therapy, exercise, diets, etc. If that's your experience, don't settle for "feeling *sort of* better." Keep trying till you feel great! Don't stop until your depression is completely gone.

How will you know when your depression is *really* gone? *Prevention* did a telephone survey of people who had overcome depression. These were the tell-tale signs of being free from depression and the percentages of people who reported each one:

- Having a good time with friends and family again (94%)
- Enjoying greater productivity at work (86%)
- Participating in activities they used to enjoy (69%)

If you're feeling better, but still don't want to go out with friends or do things you enjoy and your productivity isn't what it once was, you're not there yet—keep trying.

As many as half of the people who overcame their depression attributed their success to the fact that someone told them they *could*. So I'm telling you now: You can do it! You *can* feel better. You *can* be happy. The solution isn't the same for everyone, but your solution is out there. Don't stop looking until you find it!

GET HAPPY!

The suggestions below are from the top happiness boosters from *Self* magazine's "Editor's Picks" of May 2003. Try two of them right away and watch your mood improve!

1. Watch some really bad TV.

It works brilliantly. Just like reading a trashy summer novel, watching some really bad TV can perk you right up. It's frivolous junk food for the weary soul—calorie-free!

2. See the world from another angle.

Stand with your legs apart, then bend over and look through your legs. Check out the world around you. You're in the same place, yet everything looks different. It's a great way to remind yourself that everything can be seen from a completely different perspective.

3. Get on a swing set.

Sure, you'll feel silly at first, but that rush to your stomach as you ride on a swing is still the same. That giddy feeling of liberation is still the same too. You'll be glad to have it back, even for a moment. It helps shake things loose and give you a new start.

4. Take this advice.

OK. Here it is: "Don't compare your outsides to somebody else's insides." If you're feeling down because other people seem better off than you, think about this: How many times have you felt great, hanging out around the house on the weekend, but looked a mess? How many times have you looked like you really had your act together, on a day when you were so stressed out you wanted to scream? Surfaces can be misleading.

5. Have dessert.

Not every day. Not buckets of it. But now and then, life demands dessert. And you're entitled! Go for it!

6. Put on your PJ's.

Do it as soon as you get home from work. Maybe take a long hot shower first. Then put on your coziest, most soothing, softest flannel PJ's and leave your stress at the door.

7. Dance!

That's right—for no reason at all. Just dance. Remember Snoopy's Happy Feet Dance? Have at it. Just five minutes in the morning and five minutes when you get home at night are guaranteed to lift your spirits.

HOW TO GET OUT OF A BAD MOOD

Marjory Abrams of BottomLineSecrets.com recently sent an e-mail to her friends asking what made them laugh out loud. The top three responses? Funny movies, humor books, and joke websites.

According to researchers at the University of California, Irvine, even anticipating seeing a funny movie or video can help lift depression and boost your mood.

Funny movies

Need a list to get you going? Here are some all-time favorites:

Midnight Run
The Ref
My Fellow Americans
Crazy People
Young Frankenstein
Father of the Bride, Part II
The Life of Brian
What About Bob?
Undercover Blues

Funny websites

When you need a good laugh, check out:

www.jokepost.com
www.stupid.com

HAPPY MUSIC

Certain songs make you smile. Why not make copies and keep them nearby? Two of my favorites are Bobby McFerrin's "Don't Worry, Be Happy" and Monty Python's "Always Look on the Bright Side of Life" from *The Life of Brian.* I keep them in my car on a CD for a quick pick-me-up.

STRESS: THE HAPPINESS KILLER

When it comes to squelching happiness, one of the primary culprits is stress.

Stress is at the root of many of the illnesses and diseases we suffer from today. But long before it impairs our health, it impairs our joy. Reducing the negative effects of stress in our lives is one of the most effective ways to raise our happiness quotients.

Believe it or not, you can choose to have more happiness and less stress in your life. Are you ready to make that happen?

BOOK REFERENCE
For inspiring tips on bringing more fun into your life throughout the day, read Dr. Helen Grusd's book, *The Playful Way to Knowing Yourself* (Houghton Mifflin).

If you think about it, all of us make choices moment by moment. We choose to turn left or turn right, eat lunch now or wait until later, take the elevator or the stairs, and answer a call or let the answering machine get it. When we're not making choices consciously, our body is making choices unconsciously—to blink our eyes, to keep our heart pumping, to guarantee we're breathing, to move our leg muscles when we want to walk. Thousands of little choices make up our daily life and ultimately determine what kind of life we're living.

According to *The Doctors' Guide to Instant Stress Relief*, more than 95 million Americans suffer from a stress-related symptom every single week. Most people don't even recognize these things as symptoms. They consider them to be a normal part of life. Yet these are the very symptoms that can ruin close relationships, diminish productivity, provoke health problems, and produce the other effects that cost American businesses an estimated $150 billion a year.

SYMPTOMS OF CHRONIC STRESS

The daily stress of driving to work in rush hour traffic or juggling too many tasks at work can take a heavy toll on our physical and psychological well-being. Doctors now know that many specific physical symptoms are warning signs of too much stress. Here are just a few symptoms that can be stress-related:

Anxiety	**Anorexia**	**Chest pains**
Irritability	**Depression**	**Panic attacks**
Forgetfulness	**Diabetes**	**Irregular heartbeats**

If you have any of these symptoms, check with your doctor to uncover the root of the problem. If your symptoms are stress-related, it's even more important to actively practice stress relief techniques in your daily life to eliminate them.

HAPPY HOUR!

I strongly suggest working a "happy hour" into your life every day! Not the typical booze break, but time that you devote to making an effort to raise your spirits and "*get happy!*" The very best time to do this is on your way home from work, especially if you have had a bad day. Your spouse and family deserve the best that you have to offer when you get home. Your cheerfulness is one of the greatest presents you can bring them. It may take some real effort, but it is well worth it! The tips in this chapter will give you the tools to get you started. Don't stop there! Start a collection. Build your own happy hour kit to cheer yourself up.

THREE KINDS OF STRESS

The Doctors' Guide to Instant Stress Relief identifies three different kinds of stress:

1. **Stressful situations:** Things in our environment that provoke a stressful response in us.
2. **Mental stress:** Ways we think about things that increase our stress.
3. **Physical stress:** What we do or don't do for our bodies that increases our vulnerability to stress.

The negative impact of chronic stress is the same no matter which kind of stress it is. When you try to zero in on the situations that create the most stress in your life, start by looking at each of these areas. Are there specific ways that stress is dulling or eliminating the joy in your life?

1. Stressful situations

Think back over the last week. Can you think of five stressful situations you've encountered during that time? How about 10? If you started writing them down, could you come up with 20? During the ordinary course of a week, most of us encounter literally dozens of situations that can produce stress in our lives. Here are but a few:

- A ringing alarm clock
- A small mishap (like spilling your coffee or dropping a glass)
- Finding out the newspaper is soaking wet
- Getting up late
- Struggling to get the kids dressed for school
- Driving to work in traffic
- Running out of gas
- Having a flat tire
- Driving in the rain
- Listening to negative talk radio
- Unexpected problems at work
- Pressure on the job
- Tight deadlines
- New challenges
- Family problems
- Breakdowns in machinery or technology
- Delays of all kinds
- Interpersonal conflicts
- An illness or crisis of a loved one
- Anything that goes wrong

Sound familiar? Now that you think about it, you can probably come up with a longer list of the stressful things in your everyday life. The exercise on the next page gives you a chance to write down the major culprits. Remember: Knowledge is power. Make good use of it.

EXERCISE: IDENTIFY YOUR STRESS

Take a moment to create your own lists. Write down:

A. The ten most stressful things you've experienced this week.

1. ______________________
2. ______________________
3. ______________________
4. ______________________
5. ______________________
6. ______________________
7. ______________________
8. ______________________
9. ______________________
10. ______________________

B. The five most stressful things you've experienced today.

1. ______________________
2. ______________________
3. ______________________
4. ______________________
5. ______________________

C. Any three stressful things you've experienced in the last few hours.

1. ______________________
2. ______________________
3. ______________________

In this exercise, the magnitude of the stresses you identified may vary, but the prevalence of stressful situations was probably far greater than you expected. Starting to notice stress *as* stress when it occurs is a good first step. It is possible to nip stress in the bud before it builds up into something more damaging to your health and your life. The trick is, you have to *notice it* first!

Over the years, I have learned how important quiet time is to me. I get up by 4:30 A.M. and spend the first 30 to 45 minutes of my day in quiet time. I used to set the coffee maker with a timer so it was ready when I got up, but after reading all of the benefits of green tea, I now start the day with eight ounces of iced green tea instead. The coffee comes later.

I sit in my favorite chair in the dark, and enjoy a form of sensory deprivation. It is very quiet at that time of day, which gives me a chance to think clearly and outline everything I need to do that day. I can clear my head of any distractions.

This quiet time in the mornings is the best time of my day. I do my best thinking. Then I get up and write down everything that came to mind. It allows me to start each day with a purpose and commitment to accomplish my goals.

I can't imagine getting up and having to rush to work without having my day clearly thought out and organized, but I fear that many people function that way. It is no wonder that stress levels are so high and people are unproductive much of the time. If you don't feel in control of your time and life, try adding a period of quiet time in the morning, even if you have to get up early to do it.

BOOK REFERENCE

Peace and quiet—a rare experience in our fast-paced world—can be one of the most soothing antidotes to stress. "If you don't spend enough time by yourself, you're apt to become irritable, even depressed," says Ester Schaler Buchholz, Ph.D. For ways to make the most of your time alone, read her book, *The Call of Solitude* (Simon & Schuster).

2. Mental stress

How stressed out would you feel if someone took you up in a plane and pushed you out the door at 20,000 feet—even if you did have a parachute on? Pretty stressed, if you'd never jumped out of a plane before, but not as stressed if you were a professional skydiver.

How about public speaking? Is it stressful to give a presentation to a crowd of 1,000 people or not? Public speaking is often said to be one of many people's worst fears. If you're in that group, then it would be likely to stress you out. If you're a motivational speaker who loves sharing his insights with a crowd, you'd love it.

Experience is a factor in each of these examples. Apart from their initial attraction to skydiving or public speaking, each of these professionals has done it many times. Excitement and enthusiasm can produce stress hormones too, but the mental stress experienced by these professionals is still much lower than it would be in someone who's deathly afraid of public speaking or leaping from a plane.

While some situations are inherently stressful, it's also true that our mind can make *anything* stressful. As discussed in the last chapter, it all depends on your point of view. Notice how each of the situations below can be made stressful if you think about it a certain way.

A child's ball comes flying over the fence into your yard.

Thought #1: *That kid is nothing but trouble!*

Thought #2: *Wow. Jenna has really learned how to pitch!*

It takes 45 minutes to get through airport security.

Thought #1: *These people are so inefficient!*

Thought #2: *I'm glad they're being so thorough.*

You start doing new exercises to strengthen your lower back.

Thought #1: *This is such a hassle.*

Thought #2: *I like the way this makes my back feel.*

PRACTICE KINDNESS

Kindness is one of the best ways to relieve stress and make your life both happier and longer. According to a University of Michigan study led by Stephanie Brown, Ph.D, people who kindly help a friend or neighbor even once a year are 50% more likely to outlive those who don't.

Doing a good deed is one of the best ways to boost your mood. It's also a quick way to eliminate stress, reduce loneliness, and raise your self-esteem. Dr. Richard O'Connor, a psychotherapist and author of *Undoing Depression*, says this kind of contact with others is particularly powerful. For more tips, see Dr. O'Connor's website at www.undoingdepression.com.

Negativity is more stressful than looking for the good in things. Every time you think a negative, resisting, hostile, angry, or self-pitying thought, you magnify the stress—no matter what the situation. Imagine the stress hormones bombarding your system whenever you crank up your mental stress. If it reduces your stress, looking on the bright side can literally add years to your life!

It's not true that nice guys finish last. Nice guys are winners before the game even starts.

– Addison Walker

3. Physical stress

"What we do *to* our bodies and what we do *for* our bodies often determine what our bodies will do" in response to stress.[6] When we consume too much caffeine, sugar, salt, alcohol, drugs, preservatives, or other chemicals, we create a stressful environment within our body. What we put into our system can make it harder or easier for us to cope with stress when we encounter it.

---

6 Nathan, Ronald G., Ph.D.; Thomas E. Staats, Ph.D.; and Paul J. Rosch, M.D. *The Doctors' Guide to Instant Stress Relief* (New York: Putnam, 1987).

QUICK TIP
A few seconds of mindful breathing can turn your day around. Susan Corso, author of *God's Dictionary* (Tarcher/Putnam), recommends a simple activity. Stop for a few seconds when you feel the stress coming on, and breathe mindfully, inhaling and exhaling the word *peace.*

How we take care of our body or fail to take care of it also contributes to stress. A fit, dynamic, healthy body has a wealth of resources for shrugging off stress. By contrast, a body that is fed junk food, never exercised, and lacks adequate sleep will be much more vulnerable to stress, illness, anxiety, and pain.

By actively taking steps to improve your health and eat right, you can dramatically reduce the amount of stress you experience. In a healthy body, stressful incidents will simply not have the same impact. A few dietary changes can help you to reduce stress. If you aren't already doing these things, incorporate them into your lifestyle one by one. Your body will thank you.

1. Eat every three to four hours.
2. Include more fruits and vegetables.
3. Eliminate trans and saturated fats.
4. Increase good fats, such as fish oils.
5. Avoid sugar and preservatives.
6. Drink eight glasses of water a day.
7. Get at least 30 minutes of exercise a day.

There's an old, familiar saying: "Take care of your body and your body will take care of you." Since stress can literally kill us or take years from our lives, it only makes sense to do everything we can to reduce its impact on us. Everything we experience is filtered through our senses. Caring for our body is our first line of defense against stress.

Life is like an artichoke. Each day, week, month, year, gives you one little bit which you nibble off—but precious little compared with what you throw away.

– Oliver Wendell Holmes

THE BRIGHT SIDE OF STRESS

Question: Which is more stressful? The pressure of moving to a new house or the joy of having a baby?

Answer: Moving and having a baby can be equally stressful. Exciting events can cause just as much stress as challenging events.

Short bursts of the hormones adrenaline and cortisol can enhance our ability to think and remember things. Brief experiences of stress can actually be stimulating to the body and boost the immune system.

According to Dr. Hans Seyle, we shouldn't try to avoid *all* stress any more than we would try to avoid all food, love, or exercise.[7] Studies show that those who coped well with challenges at work were more likely to report that they were in good health than those who found the challenges overwhelming. Researchers concluded that rising to meet a challenge can be good for you.

Sustained stress is the real problem. Our bodies are not meant to endure even low levels of chronic stress without relief. Dr. Bruce McEwen, the head neuro-endocrinologist at Rockefeller University, explains that long-term stress has a corrosive effect on our brain and our body.

It's important to find a variety of ways to alleviate our stress every day, so that our body can restore itself and be ready to tackle the next challenge.

The art of living is more like wrestling than dancing.

– Marcus Aurelius

---

[7] Colino, Stacey. "Healing Power of Stress," *RDHealth.*

QUIZ: THE STRESS TEST

Take this quiz to quickly rate your level of stress. How often are each of these statements true in your life? Next to each one, fill in: (1) never, (2) sometimes, (3) frequently, or (4) always.

Example: 2 I feel close to the people around me. [sometimes]

1. ____ No matter what, I have to succeed.
2. ____ I say what I think, even if it's negative.
3. ____ Every day, I feel further behind.
4. ____ I am tired.
5. ____ I can't seem to get enough sleep.
6. ____ Things at work make me feel uneasy.
7. ____ I do not feel comfortable at home.
8. ____ It's easier to keep my feelings to myself.
9. ____ Lately, I forget things I used to remember.
10. ____ I seem more irritable these days.
11. ____ I am losing interest in sex.
12. ____ Even when I try to relax, I feel tense.
13. ____ I feel like I can't stop.
14. ____ My life is out of control.

____ Total points

Ratings:

0–14	low stress
14–29	mild stress
30–43	moderate stress
44+	high stress

GET STRESS OUT OF YOUR BODY!

Even when stress is provoked by external events, it can show up in your muscles. After chasing screaming toddlers all day, you may feel a headache coming on and notice that your shoulders are as tight as fists. As you come back to your office after negotiating a difficult deal, you may feel stiffness in your back. Each of us has different vulnerabilities.

Wherever the stress tends to show up first in your body, get it out as soon as you can. What started out as a headache from tight shoulders can end up as chronic migraines. The stiff back that could be helped by a few minutes of stretching today may require a couple months of professional treatment in the years to come, if you ignore it now.

The good news is, five minutes in between meetings (or screaming toddlers) is all it takes to get some of the stress out. Start with the suggestions below. When you see how well they work, you'll come up with more on your own.

Once you get used to maintaining a physical sensation of calm and relaxation throughout the day, you'll know it's worth five minutes and feel the motivation to keep it!

FIVE TIPS FOR STRESS RELIEF

Dr. Joan Borysenko, the former director of the mind-body clinical programs at two of Harvard Medical School's teaching hospitals, considers stress relief a key to finding inner peace, as well as maintaining physical health. Her books, *Inner Peace for Busy People* and *Inner Peace for Busy Women,* are filled with valuable information on how to improve the level of contentment in our lives. Here are a few of her favorite methods for reducing stress:[8]

1. Break large tasks down into smaller ones.

Feeling overwhelmed is much more stressful than merely feeling busy. If a task seems like too much to handle, break it down into small

---

[8] Jackson, Carole. "Wonders of Our Modern World." Bottom Line's *Daily Health News.*

component parts. Then take one step at a time. Smaller individual tasks are much more manageable than one enormous task. By reducing your stress to a more manageable level, you can access your best talents and abilities.

2. Say no.

In our increasingly busy lives, it's not uncommon to feel overcommitted. As the old adage says, "If you want something done, give it to somebody who's already busy." People who manage a lot of tasks successfully are more likely to be able to make time for one more thing. But everyone has a limit. Learn to anticipate your limit, and then don't hesitate to say no when someone asks you to do one more task.

3. Meditate.

Dr. Borysenko likes to think of meditation as "mental martial arts." It is a kind of tai chi against stress, freeing up your creativity and improving your state of mind. Even a few minutes of quiet meditation a day can soothe your nerves and restore your chemical equilibrium.

4. Center yourself.

It's the difference between facing the world with poise and strength or attacking each task helter-skelter. Taking a moment throughout the day to become centered—and then returning to your center, if you momentarily get caught up in outer events—will literally change your life and dramatically reduce your stress levels.

5. Call a friend.

Have you ever felt your neck and shoulders relax, after a long day, once you started talking to a friend? Good friends can be one of the best stress relievers of all. A brief phone call with a friend can help you let go of things that have been piling up all day—even if you don't talk about the stressful things that happened.

For more tips on finding inner balance and reducing stress, check out Dr. Borysenko's website at www.joanborysenko.com.

Jeffrey Gitomer, author of *The Sales Bible*, points out that, if you want to be happy, it only makes sense to surround yourself with happy people, at home and at work. In his e-mail newsletter, he recommends making your environment as happy as possible. It's good advice.[9]

People can be a constant source of joy and happiness in our lives. In the next chapter, we'll talk about ways to ensure more happiness, joy, and satisfaction from all of your relationships.

You've got to sing like nobody's listening, you've got to love like you'll never get hurt, you've got to dance like nobody's watching, you've got to live like it's heaven on earth.

– Anonymous

[9] Gitomer, salesman@gitomer.com.

CHAPTER 4

Choosing Happy Relationships

Shared joy is a double joy;
shared sorrow is half a sorrow.

– Old Swedish Proverb

The greatest happiness in the world is better if you share it with someone. Relationships are what give our lives meaning and continuity. Psychologists tell us that our very identities are formed in relationship to other people. It is the loving gaze of a parent that first tells us who we are. It instills in us a deep understanding that we're lovable and have a special place in the world. For the rest of our lives, we continue to thrive on love.

If you look in the dictionary, you'll see that love is defined as "a strong affection for another person, arising out of kinship or personal ties." Larry Dossey, M.D., an expert on the affairs of the heart, points out that love is a lot more than that.

Love defies definition. The idea that love is "just a feeling" is outdated. We now know that love can have a direct impact on our health and longevity. Love and affection create measurable neurological and hormonal changes in our bodies.[10] No wonder it makes us happy!

Being loved and loving other people in your life creates a far greater sense of happiness and contentment. For that reason, it is

[10] Interview with Larry Dossey. (February 18, 2004). www.bottomlinessecrets.com.

extremely important to find ways to cultivate and maintain the relationships in our lives. Do you share your feelings of love with the people you are closest to, with those who matter so much to you?

If you were going to die soon and had only one phone call
you could make, who would you call and what would you say?
And why are you waiting?

– Stephen Levine

PASS IT ON!

The circle of love in your life can be a tangible presence that fills you with energy, buoyance, and happiness every day. Expressing your feelings can make it easier for others to express their own feelings. Soon you'll be sharing love and affection with people throughout the day.

Start with your spouse, but don't stop there! Make your affection known to each of your children—and even your pets. If you continue to express your feelings of love and appreciation to the others in your life who mean a lot to you—your parents, your relatives, your co-workers, your friends, and others—you will bring love to the forefront of your life.

Too many times, the love is there, but we don't tap into it. It's a little like sitting in a room with other people and leaving the lights off. Why not flip the switch and illuminate the room with light? Sometimes it's only a matter of saying something or giving someone a hug.

When love is present, it's very easy to get the current flowing. You just need to make the effort. Why don't you stop right now and express your affection to someone you love? What would happen if you spent five minutes in a surprise phone call, just to let that person know you're thinking about them and appreciating how much they mean to you?

Once you've gotten into the habit of expressing and receiving love with the people in your life, why not take it a step further? Fill up your life with love by devoting time to charitable work and meaningful civic projects. Give of yourself to others and you will receive more than you've ever dreamed of in return!

HOW TO BE UNUSUALLY HAPPY

Recently, the Josephson Institute interviewed 100 people who claimed to be unusually happy. They found that the common denominator among these people was good relationships with others.

"Despite the widespread promotion of materialism and vanity in our popular culture, wealth and beauty are simply not enough to produce happiness," Michael Josephson says. "In fact, they're not even necessary."

Bad relationships, on the other hand, are a source of anguish and unhappiness. This is true of relationships at home, at work, with families, colleagues, and friends.

Do whatever you can to ensure that your relationships are happy and you will, at the same time, ensure your own happiness.

Appreciate the people around you. Make the effort every day to tell your partner how much you care. If you're a parent, let your kids know that you're proud of them and love them. Tell your parents that you love them and appreciate what they did for you as a child. Let your friends know how much they mean to you.

As Josephson points out, one of the best ways to express your love for others is through respect. The nonprofit Josephson Institute is working to improve the world through many activities. Find out more at their websites:

- www.charactercounts.org and
- www.josephsoninstitute.org.

RELATIONSHIP COACHING

John Gray's website www.marsvenus.com provides relationship coaching through their Ask Mars/Venus program. Visit his site or call 888-627-7836 for immediate insight and help with your relationship.

LOVE IS GOOD FOR YOU

In his book *Healing Beyond the Body: Medicine and the Infinite Reach of the Mind* (Shambala), Dr. Dossey explains that the presence of love is vital to our happiness, longevity, and well-being.

It's all too easy to neglect the people we love. In small, unassuming ways, the love we share can quietly wither and drift away if we don't cultivate it. When something is so precious, we should do whatever we can to keep it vibrant and alive.

So many people let their marriages fail and their kids become strangers to them because they simply don't give these important relationships the attention they deserve. Often, the problems can be so easily corrected. But you have to address them before things go too far!

The healthiest, most hearty house plant can survive on its own for awhile, with a little sunshine and its own natural vitality. Keeping a plant at its best takes only a few minutes. Yet a lot of people let their plants die. If you water it at random and never give it any food, your plant may stay alive for awhile, even if it grows weak from neglect. At some point, though, the dirt will crack and the leaves will droop. If you continue to ignore it, you won't be able to revive it.

The same is true of relationships. They require your attention—in the big ways and the small ways. The good news is, if you learn how to make the effort, you can make your relationships thrive!

WHEN IS AN EXPENSIVE VACATION CHEAP?

When it keeps a marriage strong and avoids the need for a divorce or counseling.

Take time to get away alone with your partner, so the two of you can reconnect and build positive memories together. The average couple spends very little time alone together every day. If you really value your relationships, making the investment in extended, quality time with one another is worth every penny.

My wife and I have been taking vacations alone together every year, without kids, for over 30 years. It has kept our marriage strong.

SEX IS BETTER THAN MONEY

Would you be surprised to learn that sex (in a long-term, committed relationship) can make you feel richer? According to a new study, sex does more for your happiness than any amount of money.[11] (As a rule, money doesn't make people *unhappy*, though, so feel free to hold out for sex *and* money!)

Strangely enough, Dartmouth College economist David Blachflower and Andrew Oswald of the University of Warwick in England have managed to put an actual dollar figure on the value of sex. Since studies had already been done to show that money can make you happier, they compared the *amount* of happiness generated by regular sex to the amount of happiness generated by adding, say, $50,000 or $100,000 to your income every year.

Sex has such a strong and positive effect on happiness that they knew the results would be large dollar amounts. They soon found that if you normally have sex once a month, but you increase it to once a *week*, it's like getting a $50,000 increase in income.

Dollar for dollar, the happiest people are those having the most sex. When their study showed that married people reported having 30% more sex than the average single person, Blachflower and Oswald went a step further. They calculated that a marriage with 30% more sex would make you just as happy as getting an extra $100,000 a year!

As you might imagine, at the other end of the scale, events that actively cause unhappiness can be measured in dollars as well. Lose that weekly sex and it will cost you $50,000 a year of happiness. Get a divorce and it's like depleting your happiness by $66,000 annually.

Some psychologists point out that it's not known for sure whether people are happier *because* they're having more sex, or whether happier people *have* more sex because they're happier. As sex therapist Robert Hatfield, Ph.D., says, "Many studies confirm that people who are depressed have less sex. If you're . . . happy . . . you're more likely to have more frequent sex."

---

[11] Kirchheimer, Sid. WebMD Medical News (July 16, 2004). www.webmd.com.

While the psychologists are debating, the rest of us can happily attest that sex is one of the most enjoyable activities humanly possible. It's not too big a leap to imagine that a great sex life can boost your happiness.

Whether you calculate it in dollars and cents or everyday bliss, there's no doubt that if you improve your relationships and your sex life, you'll be *much* happier.

So, what can you do about it?

Sex is a body-contact sport.
It is safe to watch, but
more fun to play.

– Thomas Szasz, M.D.

HAVE MORE SEX!

When German researchers asked 120 adults to keep a record of how often they had sex, they discovered that those who had the most intercourse had the best cardiovascular function. Improved cardio function is associated with lower mortality, said Dr. Stuart Brody, the director of the study. So the next time you're trekking off to the gym to work on your cardio fitness, you might think about including more sex as a part of your training!

SENSATE FOCUS

Why not start here? Sex is fun under almost any conditions. Every time you add a new skill or find a new way to enhance the experience, it gets even better. This is one of my favorites.

The Sinclair Intimacy Institute DVD, entitled *The Joy of Erotic Massage*, can transform your love life. In the DVD, loving couples demonstrate advanced methods of erotic massage that are relaxing, arousing, and satisfying. Every couple will benefit from the pleasures of giving or receiving this timeless art form. You can find it at www.drugstore.com.

There's nothing better than good sex. But bad sex?
A peanut butter and jelly sandwich is better than bad sex.

– Billy Joel

SEX Rx FOR MEN AND WOMEN!

Viagra has already changed the lives of men and women around the world. Since Pfizer introduced the pill in 1998, over 133 million prescriptions have been written. In one year alone, sales reached $1.7 billion.

BOOK REFERENCE
Mars and Venus in the Bedroom by John Gray is so invaluable, it should be required reading for all couples. Check it out at www.marsvenus.com.

With sales like these, we can expect to see constant improvements in sex pills in the coming years. It's rumored that Wrigley is even developing an anti-impotence gum!

Here are a few of the hottest new products on the market for "Sex Rx." Ask your doctor if any of these would be appropriate for you.

Sex Rx for Men

Levitra. Said to be six to nine times more potent than Viagra.

Cialis. Renowned for its long-lasting effects, it's called "the weekender."

Sex Rx for Women

Viagra. Women's sexuality is more complicated than men's, but in some cases, Viagra is ideal.

Estrogen. Imbalances can cause lower libido in women.

Androgen. Only three of the ten sex steroids are estrogen. The other seven are androgens. Correcting imbalances often solves the problem.

Sex lies at the root of life, and we can never learn to revere life until we know how to understand sex.

– Havelock Ellis

The bottom line is that if there is a problem with sexual function, new alternatives are available now that were unheard of even a few years ago. Never settle for a less than satisfying sex life. Check with your doctor to see what your options are; but remember that weight loss, or maintaining normal weight, healthy diet, and exercise will do wonders and may eliminate the need for prescription drugs.

Sex is not the answer. Sex is the question. "Yes" is the answer.

– Swami X

LOVE IN A DIFFERENT BOTTLE

My wife and I have been together for over 30 years, so gifts on holidays have become somewhat predictable. But last Valentine's Day, my wife surprised me.

As we have been doing for years, we went away for a romantic weekend in Carmel on Valentine's Day. I have always looked forward to that weekend and enjoyed it very much. But, to tell you the truth, I was expecting it to be the way it had always been—no surprises.

Then, one morning my wife insisted that we take a walk on the beach. I was happy to go along. As we walked, she suddenly stopped to give me a hug and we noticed a beautiful bottle on the beach near my feet. We could see that it had a note in it, so we opened it.

The note was from my wife.

THE POWER OF LOVE NOTES

We just can't tell each other enough how much we love each other and care about each other. A note on the refrigerator, in the car, or on a nightstand can do wonders for keeping affection flowing. Few things are more sad to me than hearing about someone having an Internet romance on the computer when their partner is in the next room, craving the kind of attention that's being given to a stranger!

If you truly love the person you're with, let them know it! Why start looking for new, stimulating experiences, when you haven't even explored the rich possibilities in the relationship you have?

It had a lovely message about how much I meant to her and how much she loved me. I was so touched that I have kept the bottle near my desk as a constant reminder.

It's such a good idea that it's become available commercially as well. If you can't find a lovely, inspiring bottle of your own, it's now possible to buy bottles for just this purpose. Special bottles and parchments for romantic moments like these can be ordered from www.timelessmessage.com You can write the note or choose from many of theirs. Having experienced the joy and surprise of a moment like this, I can tell you, it's a wonderful idea!

Remember, we all stumble, every one of us.
That's why it's a comfort to go hand in hand.

–Emily Kimbrough

MARS & VENUS

John Gray has give couples a tremendous gift by explaining the differences between men and women in simple, easy-to-understand terms. In his first book, he said it is as if men are from Mars and women are from Venus. People of both genders, all around the world, immediately knew what he meant!

Now we know how easy it is to misinterpret each other. We come from very different points of view. It's easy to fall into negative or judgmental thinking. Gray's inspired idea was to ask men and women to pretend they are from different planets. They don't come from the same world, don't share the same assumptions, and don't speak the same language.

If you start there, you're much more likely to do what it takes to really communicate and understand each other. Instead of taking certain basic things for granted, you know from the start that you're from different worlds. In my own relationship, this advice has helped both of us to be more patient, understanding, and nonjudgmental with one another. We've learned to see and accept our differences for what they are.

How we see ourselves

According to Gray, men and women base their sense of self on different things.

As a rule, men find their identities in the results they achieve at work, the things they do in the world. We like things to be concrete. We want to finish it, then step back and look it over. We like to be able to point to something and say, "I did that!" We take pride in the end result.

In other words, men tend to define themselves and prove themselves through their actions. Because of that, it's important for us to develop power and tangible skills.

> "Martians value power, competency, efficiency, action, achievement, and accomplishment. They enjoy fulfillment primarily from achieving results and doing an excellent job. Men tend to be more interested in objects and things."[12]

It was much easier for men to fulfill this instinct when they could "provide and protect" their mates and leave it at that. Over centuries of evolution, however, things have become a little more complex. Today, men are asked to do more than provide and protect. They're expected to nurture and support emotions as well.

Women, according to Gray, tend to define themselves through the quality of their relationships. They glean a sense of themselves through their connection with others. It is important to their self-image that they have valuable interactions and feel comfortable in their environment. They tend to place the most value on qualities like trust, support, and communication.

The most traditional women identify themselves and their sense of fulfillment with their ability to share, collaborate, and cooperate with others. They prefer not to do things alone, but in a group. Historically,

[12] www.marsvenus.com.

A PICTURE IS WORTH A THOUSAND WORDS

A friend of mine travels a lot and his wife has a unique way of making sure that she stays on his mind. Before he leaves on a trip, she takes a provocative picture of herself and sticks it in his luggage with a note: "I'll be waiting for you, when you get home . . ." He says that, with the photo in his luggage, he can't stop thinking about her the whole time he's away.

the men went out to provide for the family, while the women stayed home to nurture the family. Certain biological habits evolved in people of both genders during those times.

So many new choices

Today, we have more choices in how we define ourselves and find fulfillment. We also have more opportunities in this country for expressing ourselves regardless of gender. Women today are able to work and achieve their own powerful results. Achievements have become as essential a source of their identity as they once were for men.

Similarly, men are discovering the deep rewards of developing relationships, communication skills, and community. As a result, they are experiencing a new pride and sense of identity from relationships that was less available to previous generations.

John Gray's website (www.marsvenus.com) offers countless tips, quizzes, articles, and resources on this topic.

Oh, the comfort, the inexpressible comfort of feeling safe with a person, having neither to weigh thoughts nor measure words, but pouring them all out, just as they are, chaff and grain together, certain that a faithful hand will take and sift them, keep what is worth keeping, and with a breath of kindness blow the rest away.

– Dinah Craik

SINGLES IN RELATIONSHIPS

With divorce rates at an all-time high and people around the world deciding to postpone marriage, a lot of people are single. It doesn't help that dating has become more complicated in recent years. The challenge of navigating the crowded waters of the dating scene in the 21st century should not be met alone. Talk to friends. Read books. Consult websites. Do everything you can to get tips and advice. You're going to need it!

No one in the history of the world has had more options than a single person today. Ways to meet people include Internet dating, matchmaking services, and personal ads, as well as the good old standbys of meeting someone by chance or letting a friend set you up for a blind date. Videos, photos, e-mails, voicemail, text messages, video-conferencing, cell phones, and beepers add a dimension of technology that has never been known before.

The good news is, people are still the same. Relationships, for all these bells and whistles, are still the same. Some of the important rules have changed. But human nature is reliably consistent. The emotions that made us feel good 1,000 years ago are the same today.

The Mars/Venus website (www.marsvenus.com) offers these tips for women to help keep the fun in dating:

1. Date around.

You don't buy the first pair of shoes you see—you shop. It's the same with men. Don't start bonding and dreaming of the future right away. At first, it's just window shopping.

2. Don't be always available.

For centuries, men have loved the thrill of the chase. Besides that, men want women with a life. Don't be sitting by the phone waiting for his call. Get out there and do things! Be sure he hears background noise when he calls your cell. The more confident, vital, and active you are, the more interested and excited the man will be.

3. Have sex when you want to.

It's absolutely OK to wait until you are ready! If you're ready right now, that's OK too. But don't forget that sex can increase your bond and fog your brain. You may not be as objective afterward, so take that into consideration. Then wait as long or as little as you like.

4. Do not pursue a man; make him pursue you.

This is more fun anyway. In the traditional model, it was a man's job to seduce you and your job to attract him. All bets are off now. This gives you a lot more options, but one of the best ones is to get him to pursue you.

SECRETS OF SUPER-HAPPY COUPLES [13]

The very happiest couples know how to keep the daily grind of life from eroding their relationship. In a special feature, women.msn.com revealed some of the secrets that super-happy couples use to keep things fresh:

1. Fall in love again.

Treat your relationship like the romance you want it to be. If both of you work together to generate a feeling of excitement and love, you can keep the feelings flowing.

2. Keep doing what works.

The early days of most relationships are filled with romantic memories. One of the best ways to keep the daily grind from plowing your relationship under is to *keep doing those romantic things!* Go to special places together. Make new memories. Share special moments together, just as you did in the early days of your love.

---

[13] www.women.msn.com/695355.armx5-28-4.

3. Praise your partner.

Taking each other for granted is a sure-fire killer of romance. Make sure your partner knows you're not doing that by offering regular praise and expressions of love. Compliments and hugs never go out of style.

EXPRESS YOUR LOVE
The Josephson Institute provides courses, commentaries, newsletters, and articles about how to express your love in satisfying relationships. For more information visit www.charactercounts.org.

4. Look great.

Your partner may not love you for your looks, but they will always be happy to see you looking your best. Take the time to stay in shape and look your best.

5. Refrain from blame.

Blame is like a poison. Instead of pointing the finger, be playful. Lighten things up. Rent a funny movie. Replace criticism with tenderness.

6. Make time for sex.

Spontaneous sex is terrific and there's nothing wrong with having sex before you go to sleep. But in our busy lives, it's easy to cram so much into a day that you're genuinely tired by the time you go to bed. You might want to have sex, but you don't have enough energy left to enjoy it. Don't let that happen. Plan for sex if you have to, but give it all you've got.

7. Talk things out.

After you've been in a relationship awhile, it's easy to think you know the other person so well you can nearly read their mind. This can be a quick route to misinterpretations and misunderstandings. It's far better to confirm things before you make assumptions. When in doubt, just ask.

HOW CAN $2.50 A WEEK DRAMATICALLY IMPROVE YOUR MARRIAGE?

Send an "I love you" card to your spouse once a week. I have been doing it for years and it's done wonders for my marriage. This little $2.50 card has become one of the most important "messages" I communicate every week.

I keep a crazy, demanding schedule with lots of travel, but I always send a card to my wife's P.O. box so she gets it on Friday. It's a little thing, but it helps me remind her that she is the most important person in my life.

She says that what she appreciates most is not the card, but the effort I made to express my love and appreciation for her.

A great marriage is not when the "perfect couple" comes together.
It is when an imperfect couple learns to enjoy their differences.

– Dave Meurer

MARRIAGE MYTHS

Dr. Pepper Schwartz is a renowned expert on sexuality and past president of the Society for the Scientific Study of Sexuality. In her book, *Everything You Know About Love and Sex is Wrong* (Putnam), she identifies important "marriage myths":

MYTH 1: If you desire someone else, something is wrong with your relationship.

If you like sex and have a pulse, you *will* desire other people. It means you're alive, not unfaithful. Love is one thing; lust is another. There is a world of difference between desire and infidelity.

MYTH 2: Your spouse should be your best friend.

Although women often want their husbands to be their best friends, it doesn't always happen. There are many great marriages where the couples are *not* best friends. A best girl friend is far more likely to share the same point of view and enjoy talking about it than a husband. Remember, men are from Mars, women are from Venus.

MYTH 3: You should never go to bed mad.

Years ago, psychologists assumed that "letting off steam" was a good way to reduce anger. Now we know that expressing anger often makes it much worse. For one thing, it creates a surge of adrenaline and cortisol that raises your stress levels. And as often as not, listening to yourself rant simply reinforces your anger. Calling for a break is often a much better solution. Wait until you're calm to talk things over. If that doesn't happen till tomorrow morning, so be it.

MYTH 4: You should always be 100% honest.

Huge mistake. Dr. Schwartz encourages couples to think twice before they tell their partner something that creates needless worry or anxiety. The myth of confession has done a lot of harm by creating a sense of guilt when we don't share everything with our partner. In reality, the desire to "get things off your chest" can be selfish. You feel better for confessing, but your relief comes at the other person's expense.

MYTH 5: Sex that is unsatisfying can be fixed.

Not necessarily. It's possible that some of the more functional problems can be fixed, such as impotence, pain during sex, or premature ejaculation. Sexual techniques can be learned and improved. Sensitivity training and attention to sex can go a long way to make things better. But the reality is that love is not a guarantee of sexual compatibility. If the two of you are "out of sync" sexually, that may never improve.

WHY WON'T MY PARTNER CHANGE?

It's a paradox. We fall in love, and right away we want to change our partner. They're great . . . but they'd be *so much better*, if they'd only . . . !

Tim Ursiny, Ph.D., author of *The Coward's Guide to Conflict* (Sourcebooks, 2003), asks the question: When should you accept your partner's foibles, and when should you make a fuss? "There are two factors that indicate a real problem," Ursiny says. "Intensity and longevity. Does it only bother you on a bad day? Does it really only bug you a little? If either of those is true, there's no need to discuss it. But if your annoyance has a shelf life, it may be a block to your intimacy."

Being able to talk through conflicts is a crucial skill in any relationship. Psychologists often say that the ability to discuss it is more important than the conflict itself. Despite the old adage about not expecting other people to change, changes often *can* be made, with the right approach. On the other hand, if you find that you or your partner are unable to discuss the problem, it's not a good sign.

JacLynn Morris, coauthor of *I'm Right. You're Wrong. Now What?* (Sourcebooks, 2004), points out that, if you can't even get through the " 'I-need-this' talk without fighting, folding, or fleeing ... you've got major relationship issues."

A relationship is far more likely to split up because of an inability to talk things out than because he won't pick up his socks or she hangs her stockings over the shower rod. Focus on what's important—the ability to communicate—and you'll be able to work the little things out.

You know that "look" women get when they want sex? ... Me neither.

– Steve Martin

CAN YOU DECREASE TENSION IN YOUR MARRIAGE WITH A NOTE PAD?

"Men don't *listen!*" is one of the biggest complaints that women have. "It's especially hard to get them to listen, if you're asking them to do something!"

To solve this problem, I decided to make use of note pads. When my wife asks me to do something, I write it down. (For some reason, my wife is far more likely to ask me to do something if I'm in the shower. So the rule is, if I'm in the shower, *she* writes it down.)

The simple act of writing it down shows that you are listening and significantly improves the chance you'll remember to get it done. I have note pads all over the house for just that reason. It works like a charm!

LISTENING: THE CORE RELATIONSHIP SKILL

Alice Aspen March, author of *Attention: It's the Problem, It's the Solution* (www.theattentionfactor.com), points out that "positive attention is *the most valuable tool* we have for enriching the quality of our relationships. Yet it is widely misunderstood . . . and neglected."

Giving positive attention to others—especially those we love and care about—can dramatically increase the sense of connection, bonding, and understanding we feel.

In her book, March gives good advice about improving the quality of the attention you give to others. Here are a few examples:

1. Treat everyone you meet with compassion and respect.
2. Ask people what they need. Would they like you to listen or offer suggestions?
3. Embrace people's differences. Don't expect their needs to be the same as yours.
4. Look for win/win situations where both your needs and theirs are met.
5. Don't multi-task when you're in a conversation. Give others your undivided attention.

People change and forget to tell each other.

– Lillian Hellman

SECRETS OF LASTING LOVE

Falling in love is magical. Your experience of life is heightened. You walk down the street without even realizing you have a big smile on your face. Life seems full of possibility. All too often, this initial feeling of bliss subsides into something far less amenable. So what is the secret of making love last?

Dr. Ayala Malach Pines, professor of psychology at Ben-Gurion University, has studied the phenomenon of falling out of love. In her book, *Falling in Love: Why We Choose the Lovers We Choose* (Routledge Press), Dr. Pines suggests that knowing why we fell in love in the first place is the key to making love last. Here are three of her secrets for making love last:

1. Emotional arousal

A pounding heart and rapid breathing can be signs of love. Situations that evoke these effects can create an encouraging atmosphere for love. For singles hoping to meet a new mate or existing couples hoping to rekindle the flame, Dr. Pines suggests stimulating situations rather than restful ones. A hiking trip, a rock concert, or a whitewater rafting ride is far more rousing than an evening of classical music or a quiet dinner in a fine restaurant.

2. Proximity

The old saying that "absence makes the heart grow fonder" is actually a ruse. Presence makes the heart grow fonder. When we're around other people, our feelings for them intensify—for better or worse. For that reason, singles are better off meeting someone new in a class, a community group, or a local pub, where they will see each other repeatedly. Established couples must make a point of spending quality time together to stay in proximity and keep their love alive.

3. Authenticity

We all stand behind the carefully constructed personas that we need to make our way in the world. But it's a mistake to fall in love with a persona. The only way to have a true relationship with another person is to know, appreciate, and love them as they are. For single people, it's important to drop your guard and let others see you for yourself as soon as possible in a new relationship. Couples must make a point to stay authentic with one another, continuing to reveal themselves more deeply as time goes on, so the love and trust in the relationship can grow. All of us change over time, as well. Letting your partner know who you are and discovering who they are is a vital, ongoing process.

EXERCISE: EXPRESSING YOUR LOVE

Men are notoriously bad at this. Too many men think: "I told you I loved you 20 years ago. If anything changes, I'll let you know." But that just won't cut it.

When was the last time you *really* told your partner you loved them?

____

How did you communicate that (verbally; with a card, flowers, or a gift)?

____

What was their response?

____

How did that make both of you feel?

____

When are you planning to do it again?

____

How do you plan to do it the next time?

____

HOW MUCH ONE-ON-ONE TIME DO YOU SPEND WITH YOUR KIDS?

Surveys show that only 55% of dads regularly have dinner with their kids. For me, that's almost impossible to imagine. As my daughter was growing up, I made a point of coming home for dinner as often as I could.

When my daughter was born, it was one of the greatest thrills of my life. I've never forgotten that joy. Every opportunity I have to spend time with her feels like a gift to me.

From the beginning, I've always made a point to have time alone with my daughter. When she was two, I started taking her camping. Today, at 22, she still likes to go on "adventures" with her dad.

For her high school graduation, I took her to Costa Rica for 10 days. We rented a four-wheel drive, took our backpacks, and had a wonderful time. Her friends could not believe that we spent 10 full days together—and *enjoyed it!* Most of them could not spend more than 10 *minutes* with their dads.

We have climbed mountains, skied in the back-country, and camped in the snow. Our next major adventure together will be to the summit of Africa's Mt. Kilimanjaro. I've gone to see all of the traditional school sports and games she's been in.

James Dobson says that the greatest gift a father can give to his daughter is to love her mother. I wrote my daughter a letter to that effect for her eighteenth birthday, and it was very meaningful for all of us. The time that you spend with your children will come back to you in wonderful, unexpected ways throughout your life.

Let us be grateful to people who make us happy; they are the charming gardeners who make our souls blossom.

– Marcel Proust

YOUR WORK AFFECTS YOUR RELATIONSHIP—SO LOVE IT!

Love is so closely linked to our quality of life that it is important for us to spend as much time possible in a loving frame of mind every day. That means, we need to love our jobs. We spend so much time at work every day. If we don't love our jobs, that time is spent devoid of love. It drains and depletes our energy and does nothing to promote our health. Paying the bills alone isn't worth it, when we could be doing a job that directly contributes to our happiness!

EXERCISE: ARE YOU HAPPY IN YOUR JOB?

What do you like most about your present job/career?

1. ______________________________
2. ______________________________
3. ______________________________
4. ______________________________
5. ______________________________

What do you like least?

1. ______________________________
2. ______________________________
3. ______________________________
4. ______________________________
5. ______________________________

What would you change, if you could?

Ask yourself how you can spend more time doing what you like (and are probably best at), and less time doing things you don't like. Go ahead and dream. If you could change five things, what would they be?

1. ______________________________
2. ______________________________
3. ______________________________
4. ______________________________
5. ______________________________

What can you do about it?

Now, look at it realistically. Can you put your time to better use by delegating some of the "chores"? Can you improve your time management skills to get the least enjoyable things done faster or more efficiently, and move on to the more enjoyable ones? Can you renegotiate your job responsibilities or reinvent your position? List five specific steps you can take to alter the situation.

1. ______________________________
2. ______________________________
3. ______________________________
4. ______________________________
5. ______________________________

Whatever solutions you choose, make sure they allow you to get the *passion* back in what you do.

Over the course of my own life, I have reinvented my job and my position several times. Each time, it not only resulted in greater job satisfaction for me, but my reinvention became a model for others in my position around the country. Everyone wants to be happy. When they see someone else taking the initiative to make things work better, it can inspire them to do the same.

Passion is the key! You simply *must* find a way to become passionate in your work and in your relationships. It will give you a reason to get up and get going in the morning.

All of the tools and useful advice in the world won't do you any good if you don't put your whole heart into it. If you will bring more love, enthusiasm, and passion to the most important relationships in your life, your level of happiness will soar.

CHAPTER 5

Choosing to Manage Your Time

I think the world today is upside-down because... we have no time for our children. We have no time for each other. There is no time to enjoy each other and the lack of love causes so much suffering and unhappiness.

– Mother Teresa

It is one of the ironies of modern life that we have more opportunities, more luxury, more "quality of life" at our fingertips than ever before, yet we have rarely been so stressed out. We've already seen that stress can powerfully diminish our sense of happiness.

A sense of balance and control is vital to your deepest well-being. When life is reeling out of control, no one can feel happy. There is no question about it: Learning to manage your time is vital to living a happy life.

Until you value yourself, you will not value your time. Until you value your time, you will not do anything with it.

– M. Scott Peck

A STRATEGIC PLAN FOR HAPPINESS

So many things can improve our experience of happiness. Good friends, loving family members, close co-workers, satisfying activities, and accomplished goals are only a few of a host of things that can enhance our positive feelings.

Why not increase the likelihood of your happiness? Why not set your goals for happiness and make a strategic plan for bring more of it into your life?

- **Set a goal to increase your happiness.**

You know the things that increase your happiness quotient. If they don't spring immediately to mind, look back over your life and write down the moments you've enjoyed the most. Consider the big events, but don't neglect the small ones as well.

Everything from a genuine smile exchanged with a stranger to an unexpected act of kindness from a friend can cheer you up and restore a sense of well-being to your life. These are the moments that give us an overall sense that life is good and other people are deeply decent.

It's as important to cultivate these little moments in your life as it is the big, life-changing events like a child's college graduation, the birth of a new child, or an unforgettable evening with someone you love. And it's equally important to consider what you want less of in your life.

- **Set a goal to eliminate negativity.**

Have you ever gone to corner newspaper stand where the proprietor seemed to be a war with the world? Have you ever noticed that some people live from one crisis to another and there's always someone to blame? Have you ever gotten the impression from the prime time evening news that all that happened around the world today was murder and bloodshed?

This kind of negativity is poison.

The proprietor at the corner may have built a life on unhappiness, but you don't have to. The person who lives in crisis, blaming others, may live in a state of fear and distrust, but you don't have to. The news director at the television network may believe that only death and mayhem will keep the viewers' interest, but you know better. And there's no reason to allow this kind of thinking to have a presence in your life.

You know the truth: that life is good. You know that somewhere out there, while the proprietor rails against the world, there is a college student, working hard to get good grades and make something better of his life. For every person blaming others there is a kind-hearted soul making time for the small heroic acts that make up some people's everyday lives. For all the violence and mayhem in the world, there are far more good things that happen every day than bad. There's far more generosity, compassion, good-heartedness, and love in the world than will ever show up on prime time news.

How much of it you bring into your life is up to you.

All of us can be spiteful, mean, and hateful. We can all see the worst in people. It takes more effort to enact a strategic plan for happiness, but the rewards cannot be underestimated.

Deliberately change your life for the better.

Make a point to be mindful of your thoughts. Notice what kind of emotions you generate in your life. It's possible—indeed, imperative—to consciously adopt positive attitudes, like enthusiasm, appreciation, optimism, and hopefulness.

In his newsletter at www.josephsoninstitute.org, Michael Josephson encourages readers to resolve to be less cynical and assume the best, not the worst, about other people. Resist the temptation to view the world through dark lenses.

And remember that happiness and fulfillment involve more than having fun and pleasure. To optimize your strategic plan, look for opportunities to make a significant long-term, positive contribution to the lives of other people.

EXERCISE: MY FAVORITE THINGS

My personal trainer suggests this exercise to help you focus on the things that you enjoy most. Make a list of your favorite things. Then, next to each item, jot down the last time you actually did it. If it has been too long, you probably need a break. Life is too short. Take time to do the things you love!

The best way to feel good is to BE good.

– Michael Josephson

The environment you fashion out of your thoughts, your beliefs, your ideals, your philosophy is the only climate you will ever live in.

– Stephen Covey

RUSHED AND UNHAPPY

Having too much to do and too little time is a global problem. In the modern world, we're bombarded with information all day long, from e-mail to voicemail, faxes, and overnight deliveries. Everything comes faster and bigger and brighter than it used to. There seems to be a constant increase of jobs, projects, interruptions, problems, opportunities, and meetings. We'd like to pick and choose between them, but sometimes it's all we can do to keep up as we move from one thing to the next.

No matter how harried we feel, we're aware that it would take even more time to stop, get centered, and concentrate on our goals. It's far more likely that we've completely lost track of the short- and long-term goals we've set for our life.

All we know is we met the latest deadline, staved off the latest disaster, put out the latest fire, and went to bed—only to get up tomorrow to the sound of a screeching alarm and do it all again. As Jeffrey Mayer points out, our modern lives are like quicksand: "The more we struggle, the deeper we sink."[14]

It's not because we are any less adept at managing our time than our parents or grandparents were. It's because, in the Information Age, our lives have become immeasurably more complex. And the truth is, most of us haven't developed the skills we need to manage all these new demands. As time management specialist David Allen points out:

---

[14] Mayer, Jeffrey. www.succeedinginbusiness.com newsletter (July 2004).

> "Neither our standard education, nor traditional time-management models, nor the plethora of organizing tools available, such as personal notebook planners, Microsoft Outlook, or Palm personal digital assistants (PDAs) have given us a viable means of meeting the new demands placed on us … The ability to be successful, relaxed, and in control during these fertile but turbulent times demands new ways of thinking and working."[15]

It isn't that we need more time. (And even if we did, we're not likely to get it!) It's that we need to manage our lives to adapt to all of the new demands on our time. Most of us have too much to do and not enough time to do it. In order to get things accomplished, we have to make tough choices about what we can do and what we don't have time to do.

Science makes it clear that time is not actually linear. It goes more slowly in some places than in others and it is not nearly as fixed and immovable as we assume. But until they come up with a way for us to make use of that information and tune time to our preferences, we're stuck with it as it is. Time will not adapt to us. We have to adapt to time.

Since we can't manage time, we have to manage ourselves. Susan Cullen of Quantum Learning Solutions says, "If time seems to be out of control, it means that we are out of control. To bring ourselves back under control, we must learn new, more appropriate habits."

Don't say you don't have enough time. You have exactly the same number of hours per day that were given to Helen Keller, Michelangelo, Mother Teresa, Leonardo da Vinci, Thomas Jefferson, and Albert Einstein.

– H. Jackson Brown

[15] Allen, David. *Getting Things Done* (Viking, 2001), p. 7.

THE POWER OF RITUALS

Give yourself the advantage of building rituals into your life. It's always much harder to get a new ritual started than to continue something you're in the habit of doing.

If you do something for 28 consecutive days, it's more difficult *not* to do it the next day than it is to do it.

When I first started taking vitamins and eating ground flaxseed twice a day, I had to consciously make myself do it. Now I do it without thinking. If for some reason I don't, I feel like something's "off."

The same thing happened when I decided to do 75 minutes of circuit training every other morning. I had to set my alarm for 4:30 A.M. to have time in my day for a workout. So, as you can imagine, the first few days were hard. I have created a whole ritual of everything that I do before I go to the gym, so that I can fit it into an extremely busy schedule.

I can't tell you that it's gotten easier. Four-thirty is still early. And working out is still hard work. But the ritual makes it seem like a natural part of my life. It helps eliminate my resistance.

Put rituals to work for you!

The bad news is time flies. The good news is you're the pilot.

– Michael Althsuler

FOUR BASIC STEPS FOR REACHING YOUR GOALS

1. Get it off your mind.

If it's on your mind, you're distracted. You can only do one thing at a time. Any energy you take away from that thing reduces your focus and divides your energy. By writing down your goals, you keep them in a safe place till you need them.

2. Define your goals.

How can you get there if you don't know where you're going? Your basic bodily functions—like inhaling, exhaling, the beating of your heart—will happen whether you plan for them or not, but just about everything else has to be planned to be accomplished.

3. Create action steps for every goal.

Curiously enough, a lot of people leave this step out. They create a goal, such as going to Hawaii on vacation next summer or spending more quality time with their kids, then give absolutely no thought to the steps they'll take to achieve it.

To create your action choices, ask yourself, "How do I get there from here?" If the answer begins with, "As soon as I win the Lotto . . ." you're on the wrong track. What can you do *next* from where you are *now?*

Going to Hawaii next summer may mean you have to save some money every week between now and then. It will almost certainly mean arranging transportation and a place to stay.

> **BOOK REFERENCE**
> David Allen's book, *Getting Things Done* (Viking, 2001), can change your life. It's a wonderful resource of fresh ideas and specific information about organizing your life. For his excellent workshops and classes, visit www.davidco.com.

Spending more time with your kids isn't a one-shot deal either. When are your kids around? What do they have planned? How can you match up your schedule with theirs? What kinds of things can you do that they'd enjoy as well? Mentioning your plan to your kids is a good idea too.

Don't assume you'll handle it all as you go. Writing it down gets it off your mind. Breaking it down into action choices makes it manageable and deliberate.

4. Create reminders for the action steps.

There are wonderful software programs to help you do this now. Post-it notes are a good idea, but they have their limitations.

Creating a solidly organized, reliable system for tracking your progress toward your goals and managing your time along the way is the *make-it-or-break-it* step.

If you don't do this, you'll only be able to accomplish as many things as you can remember to do in the course of your otherwise busy day. Why risk it? There are ways to put a great system in place.

> *Don't be fooled by the calendar. There are only as many days in the year as you make use of. One man gets only a week's value out of a year while another man gets a full year's value out of a week.*
>
> – Charles Richards

Goals are great, but follow-through is what counts!

Reaching goals takes a lot more than making a list. Even the most exacting list won't get you any closer to your goals. You've got to have the determination, focus, and dedication to take control of your own life and do the things that matter to you. You are responsible for your own happiness, health, and wealth. It's completely up to you.

One of the world's most inspiring life stories of a man's determination to reach his goals is told in Lance Armstrong's book, *Every Second Counts.*

> "If you want to do something great, you need a strong will and attention to detail. If you surveyed all the greatly successful people in this world, some would be charismatic, some would be not so; some would be tall, some would be short; some would be fat, some would be thin. But the common denominator is that they're all capable of sustained, focused attention."

WEB REFERENCE

If you keep trying but failing to get the results that you want, check out www.in-joy.com. This website offers great insight into how to deal with poor results by identifying and overcoming the real problem.

WHY AREN'T MORE PEOPLE SUCCESSFUL?

One reason: They do not pursue specific goals. That's it.

Most of the time, people stay busy, moving from one task to the next, but they fall prey to a dangerous assumption that costs them everything: Things will work out by themselves. Things *don't* work out by themselves. Someone *makes* them work out.

CREATING ACTION CHOICES

Now it's time to make action choices. David Allen offers four criteria to help you in this process:[16]

1. Context
2. Time available
3. Energy available
4. Priority

1. Context

Where will the actions take place? This is the physical context for the action. Each of your action choices should be placed in a category, depending on where it takes place. It helps make your action concrete.

Some categories include: at the office, at the computer, on the phone, at the store, errands, etc.

Avoid at all costs a category called miscellaneous. When will you be in a location called miscellaneous? Never. It's a vague, non-specific catch-all that reinforces the tendency to just throw everything into a basket and ignore it. Getting specific is the point of action choices. Think of miscellaneous as the enemy.

2. Time available

This one seems obvious, doesn't it? But it isn't. Labeling your action choices with an estimated (or, preferably, an exact) amount of time needed allows you to get a lot more done.

[16] Allen, David. *Getting Things Done* (Viking, 2001), pp. 192–195.

If your plane is delayed for 30 minutes at the airport, you can look at your list of action choices and choose the things that fit into both the context of the airport (reports to read, speeches to write, calls to make, meals to eat) and the time available.

As Allen says, the most productive way to get the short things done is to make use of the little "weird time windows" that are scattered throughout the day.

3. Energy available

Keeping things off your mind and knowing exactly what you're going to do every day will allow you to pace yourself—which will, in turn, help you make the best use of your energy. But there's only so much energy to work with. Consistent eating habits have a direct impact on energy. The types of food we eat make all the difference. Rest is vitally important.

When you're tired, even the smallest tasks seem overwhelming. It's important to know as much as you can about the kind of energy you can rely on. How much does a two-hour presentation usually take out of you? Do you feel energized afterward or in need of a nap? How much energy will you have if you get in 30 minutes of cardio in the morning? How much energy will you have if you don't?

When you know yourself and your energy patterns well, you can begin to realistically anticipate how many things you can do throughout the day. Then you can schedule different tasks to match the level of energy you're likely to have.

QUICK TIP Jeffrey Mayer reminds us to take a look at our To-Do lists. Consider each item and ask yourself: *"Is this activity going to help me reach my goal?"*

- If the answer is yes, think of ways to do it faster, better, and less expensively.
- If the answer is no, then STOP doing it!

Visit www.succeedinginbusiness.com to check out his new training manual.

Are you a morning person who hops out of bed at their best? Or do you really hit your peak around mid-afternoon? Schedule low-energy activities, such as reading the paper or watering the plants, for low-energy times, and save the high-energy activities for times when you'll be at your best.

4. Priority

Establishing priorities among your action choices is vital. If something has to be done by 2:00 P.M., that's a significant piece of information. When it comes to deadlines, priorities are easy to establish. The action choices can be arranged according to the clock.

In other areas, however, the choices aren't so easy. Often our priorities are determined by our personal values and responsibilities.

It may be hard to imagine in your busy life, but if you came home from work at 7:00 P.M. and had the evening free, what would you do? Something active and fun? Something with someone you love? Or would you crave a couple hours by yourself in the jacuzzi?

Knowing the four basic criteria—where you are, what kind of time and energy you have, and what your priorities are—will help you make a decision you'll be happy with.

> *There are risks and costs to action. But they are far less than the long-range risks of comfortable inaction.*
>
> – John F. Kennedy

MAKE CUMULATIVE GOALS

Most of your goals should be progressive. One should lead to another. Daily goals should lead to weekly goals, to monthly goals, to yearly goals, to five-year goals, and so on. For example, saving $50 a week leads to $215 a month, then $2,600 a year.

If you save $50 a week, but spend it every week, you're getting nowhere. As often as possible, make your goals cumulative. It's the nature of life that we can only take one step at a time, but if we do it right, the results in the long-term will be amazing!

HOW CAN YOU BEST LEVERAGE YOUR TIME? [17]

We all have limited time to do what's important to us. How can you leverage your time to get the most out of it? Here are three tips:

1. **Block out time for yourself every day.**

   Do not answer the phone or e-mail. Do not accept any interruptions. This is your time. Do what you will with it.

2. **Only do what matters.**

   Put first things first. Then eliminate as much of the rest as possible. Only do what's important.

3. **Use your best time wisely.**

   Do you find you have more energy at a certain time of day or night? Use it to your advantage. Do the projects that require the most energy and enthusiasm in that time period, if you can. You'll get more out of every minute that way.

In truth, people can generally make time for what they choose to do; it is not really the time but the will that is lacking.

– Sir John Lubbock

EXPECT THE UNEXPECTED

Let's face it, you're going to be interrupted.

No matter how airtight your schedule is tomorrow, things are not going to go exactly according to plan. It's not your fault. It's life. An android could make a schedule and they'd still run into interruptions. That's just the way things are.

You may not have control over all the interruptions in your life. But to some degree, you can expect the unexpected.

---

[17] Mayer, Jeffrey. www.succeedinginbusiness.com newsletter (July 2004).

When you're writing down your list, leave a little air. *Plan* for interruptions. If you schedule every minute of your day, you're living in a fantasy. You *will* be interrupted. Unexpected things *will* happen. So allow for them. And when they happen, write them down.

What interrupted you? When? How long was the interruption? Before long, if you check back, you may notice a pattern that will allow you to make important changes. Save yourself an hour a day and in less than a month, you'll have added 24 hours to your life!

WEB REFERENCE

For a website brimming with all kinds of great advice on goals and how to achieve them, check out The GoalsGuy website: www.goalsguy.com. It offers a complete suite of performance improvement solutions, including:

- A library of handbooks.
- World-class e-resources in real time to any location around the world.
- High-impact training programs to enhance your productivity and performance.
- TeleSeminars over the phone, on performance improvement topics.
- Keynote speeches that energize, inspire, and motivate performance.
- One-on-one coaching designed to increase your sense of direction, confidence, and results.
- A free newsletter that is affectionately known as "a weekly manifesto of thought-provoking insights and ideas."

Lost wealth may be replaced by industry, lost knowledge by study, lost health by temperance or medicine, but lost time is gone forever.

– Samuel Smiles

PUT YOUR RETICULAR ACTIVATING SYSTEM TO WORK FOR YOU

In 1992, when Anthony Robbins came out with his enormously successful book, *Awaken the Giant Within*, few people knew much about the reticular activating system in the brain. In his own inimitable way, Tony Robbins brought the power of this wonderful, organic tool within us to light. He wrote:

> "Once you decide that something is a priority, you give it tremendous emotional intensity, and by continually focusing on it, any resource that supports its attainment will eventually become clear . . . Trust that your [reticular activating system] will point out what you need to know along the way." [18]

But exactly what is the reticular activating system (also known as RAS) that Robbins is talking about? And why is everybody so excited about it?

Tap into the motivational center of your brain

People get excited about RAS for good reason. It is one of the primary motivational centers of our mid-brain. In daily life, it is the RAS that determines whether we're feeling highly motivated or bored. Most importantly, it helps us reach our goals.

The RAS is the part of the brain that helps us focus on a goal, make decisions that take us toward that goal, and find every resource possible to help us achieve that goal. In that way, it is the key to our success.

---

[18] Robbins, Anthony. *Awaken the Giant Within.* p. 288.

If you make a clear goal, the RAS will help you reach it. If you're not quite sure of all the details but make a clear goal to find out the details, the RAS will get to work on it.

The RAS and your new house

Suppose you want to buy a new house. They've built an airport near your neighborhood and the planes are keeping you awake at night, so you know you've got to move, but you don't have any particular goals in mind. You thumb through the real estate ads in the paper, but don't really find anything. Maybe you even talk to a realtor or two, but nothing really strikes your fancy. Why? Because you don't have anything specific in mind.

> **WEB REFERENCE**
> Success Studios has produced new software called GoalPro 6.0, which is said to be the finest software-based goal-setting system available. Check it out for yourself. You can find a free product tour and free 30-day trial version: www.goalpro.com.

Take a few minutes to think about what you want in your next house and everything changes. You know you want certain things: a quiet neighborhood, a residential street with well-kept lawns, a certain number of bedrooms, a kitchen of a certain size, maybe a garden or a pool. As your concept takes shape, your enthusiasm begins to grow. Suddenly, this new house is starting to appeal to you! Your RAS is beginning to respond.

Before long, you start noticing houses that may fit your qualifications as you drive down the street. You start plugging realtors' phone numbers into your PDA, as you pass their signs on the streets. Your weekends fill up with visits to open houses. Within an astonishingly short period of time, you've found exactly what you're looking for!

In fact, *this* house has things you didn't even realize you wanted—the perfect wall for your big-screen TV, an extra room in the back for a home office, even a blooming calla lily (your favorite flower) by the door. Some people might call this a supernatural sign. In reality, it's just your reticular activating system going to work for you—checking everything out, putting things together, helping you achieve your goals more thoroughly than you'd even imagined!

Making history with RAS

On his website, Bob Choat writes about Albert Einstein and RAS:

> "When he was still a child, Albert Einstein wanted to know what caused objects to behave the way they do. He kept this focus throughout his life. He remained a perpetual child —in the sense that he was always excited about the possibilities of the universe. He always asked himself questions and sought to have them answered. Everything around him stimulated his RAS to finally create the Theory of Relativity."

The reticular activating system function of the brain will operate on our behalf whether or not we know anything about it. But the process of setting clear goals stimulates the RAS like nothing else. Why not use it to your benefit?

Joseph Campbell famously encouraged people to "follow their bliss." One day, he explained to an audience the reasons for doing it. He said it's not just that closed doors will open for you if you go after what you love in life, but the amazing thing is that doors will open that *weren't even there before.* That's the reticular activating system at work—finding new ways to help you, ways you didn't even see before.

BOOK REFERENCE
Jeffrey Mayer's book, *Making More, Working Less,* has helpful tips on time management and getting the most out of sales calls. Go to www.succeedinginbusiness.com.

For more on goal-setting and the power of the mind, see www.hypnomindpower.com: "The Why and How of Setting Goals That Can Make You Successful."

WHY SMART PEOPLE PROCRASTINATE MOST

Turns out, it's the smartest people who have the most undecided things on their minds. That's because when we focus on things we have to do, our mind calls up an image. We think of biting into a big, succulent orange with the juice dripping out and our mouth starts to water. We think of doing three loads of laundry or wading through a stack of mail and feel an immediate rush of dread and boredom.

The most creative, sensitive, and intelligent people feel the brunt of their imagination most strongly. While they have an advantage in being able to visualize their goals and bring them to life in their minds, their vivid imaginations work against them when it comes to things they don't want to do.

It's easy to imagine worse-case scenarios. Let your imagination run rampant over any task and you can quickly turn an innocent event into something well worth putting off as long as possible!

Mark Twain put it best when he said: "I am an old man and have known a great many troubles, but most of them never happened."[19]

You will never find time for anything.
If you want time, you must make it.

– Charles Bixton

WHAT IS YOUR TIME MASTERY APTITUDE?

The Time Management Report, available through Quantum Learning Solutions at www.quantumlearn.com, can give you a clear idea of your current level of time management aptitude. The company also offers a brief, interactive Internet course to teach you the most important time management skills.

All of us have strengths in different areas of time management. Having experienced it myself, I can highly recommend the Time

[19] Allen, David. *Getting Things Done* (Viking, 2001), pp. 240–241.

Mastery Profile. It will provide you with a comprehensive analysis of your strengths and vulnerabilities in important aspects of time management. The Quantum Learning Solutions skill analysis measures your skills in these specific areas:

Attitudes	Interruptions
Goals	Meetings
Priorities	Written communications
Analyzing	Delegation
Planning	Procrastination
Scheduling	Team time

The Time Management Profile points out that there are two ways to approach time mastery. You can focus on results or focus on the actions you're taking to achieve those results. Focusing on results will give you the greatest success.

Never take a meeting or engage in an activity without asking yourself: What is my goal? What result do I want to achieve? If it's a phone meeting, your goal may be to set an appointment or get approval for funding. If you're stopping by the grocery store on the way home, your goal may be to get a carton of milk.

How many times have you found that you sat down to finish a project, but then the phone rang, and then the printer ran out of paper, and then a colleague stopped by to ask a question . . . and soon three hours had gone by and you still hadn't finished what you sat down to do in the first place?

Not every unexpected event can be avoided. You can't just "power through it" if your printer's out of paper. You're going to have to fill the paper tray. No amount of determination and bravado are going to help you if you're printing on thin air.

The key is in not spending time, but in investing it.

– Stephen Covey

But often, interruptions can be minimized if you focus on results. The experts at Quantum Learning Solutions emphasize the importance of ruthlessly eliminating things that are *not* aimed at your result. It's not enough to merely do what you set out to do. You have to *not* do things you did *not* set out to do. Sometimes that's the trickiest part![20]

CREATE A THINGS NOT TO DO LIST!

Another great suggestion from Jeff Mayer is to create a list of Things *Not* to Do.

It's easy to get sidetracked by things. Often, when you do get sidetracked, you're being sidetracked by the *same old things*. So make a list of them. Then make sure you don't do them.

Here are a few examples of things it's easy to spend too much time doing:

- Talking on the phone
- Listening to negative people
- Mulling things over
- Surfing the web
- Watching TV

If you're not sure what your things are, then spend a week writing down all the times you do something that's not on your schedule for the day. Write down what it was and how long it took. At the end of the week, you'll notice a pattern. Some can't be eliminated, but others can. Put them on your Not To Do list.

These things keep you busy, but they do not help you reach your goals. They fritter your life away.

To wring the most happiness possible out of life, you have to parcel your time out carefully on those things that bring you joy, happiness, and satisfaction.

[20] Quantum Learning Solutions, Time Management Profile, www.quantumlearn.com.

As Mayer says, "Do things that lift you up, add value to your life, make you feel energized. Do things that give you great rewards and huge payoffs."[21] You'll find yourself happier than you ever thought possible.

WHEN YOUR TO-DO LIST STRESSES YOU OUT

It's a common problem when To-Do lists create more stress than they relieve. Instead of keeping us focused, they degenerate into guilty reminders that overwhelm us. As the day goes on and we don't find time for some of the items on the list, it starts to undermine our confidence.

Ideally, a To-Do list should be a source of clarity for productive action. But all too often it's more like salt in the wound, drawing our attention to decisions we've avoided, conversations we've put off, and things we haven't managed to fit in.

It's important to be realistic about these lists. Constantly remind yourself that you can only do one thing at a time. The list itself is made of one item at a time. Put down everything that you need to do, organize the items, and accomplish them to the best of your ability. While you're working at each item—whether it's personal or professional—don't divert your energy to *anything else*. And you'll work your way through the list.

To learn new techniques for improving your time management and organizational skills every week, subscribe to David Allen's enewsletter@davidco.com, "A Smarter Way to Work and Live."

WHY DO WE PROCRASTINATE?

It's on your schedule, looking right at you: 7:30—go to the gym. You're awake. You've had your coffee. On a good day, you've even

[21] Mayer, Jeffrey. www.succeedinginbusiness.com newsletter (July 2004).

gotten dressed for the gym . . . but you're hanging around the kitchen counter, thumbing through the paper, fiddling with your keys . . . It's already 7 o'clock. The gym is 10 minutes away, so you do have a little while longer. But what are you waiting for? Why do you put it off?

No one forced you to write "7:30—go to the gym" on your schedule. This is a schedule of things you want to do. Right?

So why do you procrastinate? Why do any of us?

Alan Lakein, renowned time management consultant and author of *How to Get Control of Your Time and Your Life,* says that procrastination is often based on one of two things. The thing we're procrastinating about is usually:

1. Overwhelming, or
2. Unpleasant.

Fortunately, there are solutions. Lakein offers great advice for overcoming procrastination and moving through our schedule smoothly.

What to do when the task is overwhelming:

- Break it into action steps.
- Do it now, but ease into it. If you can promise yourself you'll at least try it for *five minutes*, you'll be over the hurdle. (Once you get started, it's usually not as bad as you thought.)
- Remind yourself of the benefits. There was *some reason* it was on your list, right?
- Warn yourself about the negative consequences of *not* doing it!
- Set a final deadline and do it, no matter what, before that time.

What to do when the task is unpleasant:

- Again, do it now, not later. Put it behind you.
- Warn yourself of how much worse it will be if you *don't* do it.
- Remind yourself that, ultimately, you're going to have to do it anyway. Would you rather spend Monday through Friday dreading it or get it out of the way by Monday afternoon?
- Offer yourself a reward for doing it.

You'll find more powerful procrastination-beaters at Alan Lakein's website. For further study, he offers a cassette or CD course: "Conquering Procrastination: How to Stop Stalling and Start Achieving." Visit www.about-goal-setting.com/procrastination.html.

Most people overestimate what they can accomplish in a year—
and underestimate what they can achieve in a decade!

– Anthony Robbins

HELP WITH GOAL-SETTING

Check out myGoals.com, the award-winning goal-setting website widely praised on CNN, ABC News, CBS, and WSJ. It is the web's leading site for setting and managing your goals. The site provides tools that "walk you through a comprehensive, step-by-step goal-setting process for any goal, whether it's short-term or long-term, easy or difficult, practical or lofty."

To give you an idea of the kinds of things people are setting and reaching goals around, here are the top 10 favorites on the site on a given day:

1. Lose 10 pounds
2. Pay off my debt

3. Become fluent in Spanish
4. Start my own business
5. Learn more about wine
6. Spend more time with my family
7. Learn to play golf
8. Read more often
9. Reduce stress in my life
10. Write and sell a screenplay

Once you've set your goal, they send you reminders via e-mail, set to arrive exactly when you should be working on the next task. *Their* goal is to keep you focused and on track to accomplish *your* goals. Some of the most popular categories include:

- **Health and fitness goals**
  Exercise, nutrition, weight loss, peak performance, cosmetic surgery.

- **Family and relationship goals**
  Friends, romance and marriage, family, people skills.

- **Time management and organization goals**
  Recordkeeping, housekeeping, creating more time, staying in touch.

- **Personal finance goals**
  Investing, paying off debt, cutting expenses, charity and philanthropy.

- **Education and training goals**
  College and grad school, job-related, K-12, languages, technical literacy.

- **Career goals**
  Job-seeking skills, education, entrepreneurship, promotions.
- **Personal growth and interest goals**
  Arts, music, writing, community, spirituality, joie de vivre.
- **Recreation and leisure goals**
  Travel, boating, golf, outdoors, cooking, dancing.
- **Home improvement and real estate goals**
  Kitchen, pool, buying a home, rental property, cabin, garden.

TAKE A 20-MINUTE GOAL-SETTING TUTORIAL

If you're new to setting goals, you'll find a wonderful 20-minute tutorial at www.about-goal-setting.com/goal-setting-tutorial.html. This hands-on tutorial will give you an actual experience of a step-by-step goal-setting process. The accompanying articles include:

The goal-setting blueprint

Step 1 Intense Desire: Rocket Fuel for When You Set Goals!

Step 2 Writing Goals Down Ties Them Up!

Step 3 To Reach Goals: Bypass Resistance and Gather Assistance

Step 4 Goal Planning: Use Deadlines As Lifelines

Step 5 Goal Objectives: Looking Ahead to Get Ahead With Planning

Step 6 When Reaching Goals Use Mental Pictures: Put an MGM Studio In Your Head!

Step 7 Achieving Goals: The Remaining 90%—Sheer Persistence

For a trial run of your own goals and objectives, with a valuable tutorial at your side, this is a great place to start.

Part 3

GET HEALTHY

The higher your energy level, the more efficient your body. The more efficient your body, the better you feel and the more you will use your talents to produce outstanding results.

– Anthony Robbins

CHAPTER 6

Choosing to Get in Shape

You may delay, but time will not.

– Benjamin Franklin

More than one billion people around the world are overweight. The World Health Organization places obesity and two illnesses closely connected to it, heart disease and high blood pressure, in the top 10 risks to global health. Obesity is responsible for at least 300,000 deaths every year. Type 2 diabetes, a common outcome of obesity, has been steadily increasing around the world.

In America, as many as 65% of adults are overweight. A decade ago that number was 56%. The percentage of overweight children is three times higher than it was in 1980. Black and hispanic women have the highest rates of obesity.[22]

Studies show that, on any day of the week, as many as 44% of adults in the United States are on a diet. The desire to lose weight is high. If losing weight was easy, millions of people would have lost weight and kept it off by now.

You don't drown by falling in the water.
You drown by staying there.

– Anonymous

[22] Grady, Denise. "Fat: The Secret Life of a Potent Cell," *The New York Times* (July 6, 2004).

The reality is that many people struggle for years to lose weight. Ironically, the people who try the hardest are often the ones who have the least success in the long run. A nutrition study done by *Self* magazine showed that people who made a point to watch what they ate, "eating light meals but sometimes splurging, yo-yoing back and forth on diets, and reducing calories by 200 a day—had a 30 percent greater chance of becoming overweight" than those who didn't focus on finding the latest diet and eliminating foods they loved. People who simply ate a consistent, moderate diet had a 22% lower risk of becoming overweight than those who dieted.[23]

There's little doubt that following the latest fad or trying to stick closely to a diet that restricts too many of the foods you love will backfire. The key is to make sound food choices you can live with. Make modest changes to your diet and make exercise a regular part of your life. As you'll see in the chapter on exercise, you can literally eat more food every day without a penalty if you exercise more.

Your body is the baggage you must carry through life.
The more excess baggage, the shorter the trip.

– Arnold H. Glasgow

The key to controlling your weight is keeping your energy intake (food/calories) and your energy output (physical activity) in balance. When you consume only as many calories as your body needs, your weight will usually remain constant. If you take in more calories than your body needs, you will put on excess fat. If you expend more energy than you take in you will burn excess fat.

The yo-yo dieters in the *Self* study may have been eating exactly the right foods and even exercising right for short periods of time. But they would've been better off to make healthy choices consistently over the years. Permanent fitness and weight loss are only possible

[23] "Shaping Your Future," ABCNEWS.go.com (August 20, 2004).

through lifestyle changes that include what you eat, what kind of exercise you do, and what mental steps you take to stay on track. Goal-setting and self-esteem are every bit as important as food and exercise. With the right mindset, your chances of making long-term changes are much higher.

ARE YOU OVERWEIGHT?

The answer is pretty straightforward. The official definition of "overweight" is a weight that is 10% above the appropriate body weight. "Obese" means a weight that is 20% over the appropriate body weight.

Increasingly, however, nutritionists and fitness experts are acknowledging that two different people at the same weight and height can have radically different fitness levels. Since muscle mass is heavier than fat, an athlete may weigh much more than someone who doesn't work out, yet be much more fit. Since fat takes up a lot more space than muscle of the same weight, a person who is out of shape is likely to be much bigger than a fit person of the same weight.

> **WEB REFERENCE**
> The Metropolitan Life standardized weight-height chart has been used for years to determine appropriate weight ranges for adults. To check your own weight, see their chart at www.trueimagefitness.com/your_ideal_weight.htm

That explains why two other percentages are being used more often: body mass index and body fat percentages.

Body mass index (BMI)

You will find any number of body mass index (BMI) calculators online. The Centers for Disease Control website makes it easy for you. To do the calculation yourself, simply divide your weight (in kilograms) by the square of your height (in meters). (To translate your weight to kilograms, multiply your weight in pounds by 0.45. To translate your height to meters, multiply your height in inches by 2.5, then divide the result by 100. Or go to www.onlineconversion.com for help making these conversions.)

A healthy BMI is between 20 and 25. A BMI that is smaller or larger is associated with significant health risks.

Obsessed is the word the lazy use to describe the dedicated.

– Anonymous

More die in the United States of too much food than too little.

– John Kenneth Galbraith

WEB REFERENCE

OnlineConversion.com boasts that they will make it easy for you to "convert just about anything to anything else." And they're right. Their instant calculators will come up with over 50,000 conversions. To convert your weight and height to the metric system, check out www.onlineconversion.com.

Body fat percentage

A registered dietitian or exercise physiologist can give you the most accurate measurement of your body fat.

One of the ways to determine body fat is by the use of a caliper. It is an instrument that will measure the thickness of a fold of skin in various parts of your body to estimate your total body fat. In America, a typical adult woman of average will have between 20 and 30% body fat. Adult men in America have an average of 10 to 20% body fat.

WEIGHT LOSS BASICS

Do the math

To a certain degree, losing weight is based on the math.

A pound of fat equals about 3,500 calories. It stands to reason that if you eat 3,500 fewer calories per week, you will lose weight.

CALCULATE YOUR BMI
The Centers for Disease Control (CDC) has a simple, online calculator that will determine your body mass index (BMI). It won't be as accurate as the measures used by a professional, but it will give you a good estimate. You can find it at www.cdc.gov/nccdphp/dnpa/bmi/calc-bmi.htm.

One way to do this is to eat 500 calories less per day. In seven days, you will have lost a pound (500 calories × 7 days = 3,500 calories). If you'd rather lose two pounds a week, reduce calories by 1,000 a day.

The math is legitimate. In reality, however, a lot of other factors influence how much weight you lose. A pound always equals 3,500 calories. But if losing weight were entirely based on math, you would be able to keep cutting calories until you lost *all* of your body weight. Fortunately, our bodies are more complicated than that!

Metabolism plays an important regulating role in weight loss. If you eat too much or too little, your metabolism changes.

To build a lean, healthy body, you HAVE to eat.

– Bill Phillips

Eat often

A classic weight loss mistake is to skip breakfast, then eat lunch and dinner. Someone who takes this approach doesn't realize that they have radically altered their metabolism by doing this. When their body perceives that they haven't eaten for almost 16 hours (from 8:00 P.M. till noon the following day), their metabolism will creep to a halt, conserving energy as if it were starving on a desert island. They would be far better off to eat smaller meals every two or three hours. The frequent meals would help keep their metabolism up.

Exercise also has a dramatic impact on metabolism. On a purely mathematical basis, it's possible to decrease your calories by 500 to 1,000 calories a day with exercise alone! The metabolic benefits of aerobic exercise have an even greater effect. Just 20 minutes of sustained exercise at 85% of your maximum heart rate can boost your metabolism for hours!

Eat enough

One important thing to remember with any calorie reduction program is that it is possible to make your diet backfire by eating *too little*. The lowest recommended intake for women is 1,200 calories per day. For men, the lowest recommended intake is 1,500 calories per day.

WEB REFERENCE
For more tips on weight loss and getting in shape, check out my website at www.gethappy-gethealthy-bewealthy.com.

Some liquid diet programs reduce calories even lower, to 500 or 800 calories per day. All of these programs should be medically supervised for safety. And the long-term metabolic effects should be considered carefully before beginning such a program.

You can't have a better tomorrow if you are thinking about yesterday all the time.

– Charles F. Kettering

WHAT'S THE BEST DIET?

The truth is, a lot of diets work. You could eat only pineapples for a month and lose weight. The All-Fruit-All-the-Time diet has a long-standing tradition that goes back to the end of the 19th century. If you stick to it, you'll definitely lose weight. Of course, you'll be irritable, a little buzzed with your heightened blood sugar, and you won't be healthy at all. Most people who go on this diet become so dizzy that they literally start walking into walls. But they do lose weight!

It's not a question of whether you can lose weight. You can. The important thing is to lose it in a healthy way and keep it off!

The best diet is the one that works for you. It is such a good fit for your tastes and your lifestyle that it becomes a permanent part of your daily routine. Any number of diets follow sound nutritional principles. You need a diet that is *also* a good fit for you.

In this chapter, I'll give you the information you need to make the choice that's best for you. Next, you'll be able to put together an exercise program that super-charges your metabolism and burns away the calories, so you can lose weight once and for all!

BOOK REFERENCE
For comprehensive, easy-to-understand information on how to create exactly the right diet for you using your body mass index and body fat percentages, get Tom Venuto's excellent book, *Burn the Fat.* You can download it right now at www.burnthefat.com.

Nothing in life just happens. You have to have the stamina to meet the obstacles and overcome them.

– Golda Meir

AVOID FAD DIETS

This may shock you, but when some people write diet books, promoting some new-fangled miracle diet that has helped people lose an enormous amount of weight almost overnight, they're just making that stuff up! They may have amazing before-and-after photos. They may quote scientific studies. And it may be that none of it has *any basis whatsoever* in reality.

Not all diet books are like that. A lot of people have lost weight on fad diets in the short term. So not all diets books have to resort to fabrication. But how can you tell the difference?

Here are a few things to look for.[24] If the diet does these things, it's most likely just a fad:

[24] "How Do I Spot a Fad Diet?" content.health.msn.com (August 1, 2004).

- Promises a quick fix
- Sounds too good to be true
- Lists "good" and "bad" foods
- Requires that you buy a lot of extra products
- Assumes all dieters are the same
- Eliminates one or more of the five food groups

A responsible diet includes nutritional balance. It acknowledges that it takes time to lose weight, and that not everyone loses weight at the same rate or with the same combination of tools. It recognizes that losing weight quickly and regaining it quickly is hard on your body, so it encourages long-term lifestyle changes instead.

Don't fall for a fad. You're better than that. Treat yourself to the best nutrition available. It's your life!

LOW-CARB OR LOW-FAT?

Is it easier for you to cut back on carbs, like pizza and pasta, than to cut back on fat? Or are you the one who always says, "I'll give up butter, but I can't give up bread!"

Right away, you're in luck. No matter what the advertisements say, low-carb diets don't work any better than low-fat diets in the long run.

For the first six months, low-carb diets (such as the Atkins diet or The Zone diet) will help you lose slightly more weight. But by the end of the year, people on a low-carb diet have lost no more weight than those on other reduced calorie diets.

EAT MORE GOOD CARBS!

A balanced diet is based on healthy carbohydrates like whole grains, beans, fruits, and vegetables. They contain fiber, so they break down slowly in your body. A slice of white bread or a chocolate chip cookie can make you crave sugar later, but high-fiber carbs won't.

Low-carb diets

Not everyone loses weight quickly on a low-carb diet. This diet works best for people who have been eating too many carbs in the first place. If you love starchy foods, like potatoes, muffins, bread, and pasta, you may see dramatic changes with a low-carb diet. If your favorite foods have a lot of sugar, like soft drinks, juices, candy, and dessert, cutting back on those high-carbs food can make a real difference in your weight.

The pros

Low-carb diets, such as the Atkins diet, have the advantage of simplicity. You don't have to remember to balance your food or count your calories. You don't have to think about portions at all. You focus on eating a lot of protein. The protein helps reduce your hunger, so it's easier to skip the carbs.

The cons

Because you don't balance your food intake on many low-carb plans, you can end up with a diet that is not nutritionally sound. In the long run—maybe sooner—your body will start feeling the effects of that unbalanced diet. If you're not eating enough vegetables, for instance, you won't be getting enough of the rich vitamins and antioxidants you need.

BEWARE THE "LOW-CARB" CANDY BAR!

Sounds good, right? Candy that's low-carb. It's like having your cake and eating it too! The truth is going to hurt. Most low-carb candy bars are full of carbs. They've simply traded the more familiar carbs with sugar alcohols, such as sorbitol, mannitol, and maltitol. These sugars can cause cramps, bloating, gas, and diarrhea.[25] Kind of takes the fun out of that candy bar, doesn't it?

[25] Erasmus, Udo, Ph.D. *Fats That Heal, Fats That Kill* (Alive Books) www.udoerasmus.com (July 5, 2004).

Nutritional deficiencies take awhile to show up, but they will impact your health in the long run. Your joints, your skin, your eyesight, and your stamina are just a few of the things that are directly affected by nutrition.

The best way to predict the future is to create it!

– Jason Kaufmann

Low-fat diets

If you reduce the fat in your diet by eating leaner meats and lower-fat dairy products, and avoiding high-fat snacks, you'll lose weight. For decades, doctors recommended low-fat diets. Fat is easily the most concentrated source of the calories we eat. And in recent years Americans have gravitated toward high-fat diets. So it only made sense that cutting back on fat would do the trick.

The pros

If a significant portion of your calories has been coming from high-fat foods, you'll lose weight by going on a low-fat diet. If you've been eating too much of anything, reducing it will help you lose weight in the short term. Reducing your overall calorie consumption is what makes it work.

The pitfall for many low-fat dieters is that they eat low-fat foods without paying attention to their calorie intake. Grocery stores are filled with low-fat versions of everything from milk to bread to pastry to chocolate bars. If you eat too many of them, you won't lose weight.

The cons

Low-fat diets often leave people feeling hungry. The fat content in food can create a very satisfying feeling. Even when the manufacturers have perfected the taste, the experience of eating a low-fat donut is not the same as eating the full-fat version.

Luckily, nature has provided us with the perfect solution: whole foods. The colorful, vitamin-rich bounty of foods in the produce section of your neighborhood market is filled with foods that will satisfy your hunger and make you healthier at the same time! Fruits, vegetables, and whole grains such as rice, barley, quinoa, and wheat are very filling.

Eating foods that are nutritious and well-balanced is the best way to get healthy and get in shape. Doing it for two months before bikini season isn't the answer. Learning to love it enough to do it the rest of your life is the only way.

QUICK TIP
Beware of meal replacements. Those 250-calorie drinks you mix with water and chug down when you're in a hurry can cost you later. If you eat too little during the day, you may compensate by eating too much later!

THE BAKED POTATO TEST

Which would you rather cut back on: carbs or fat?

One of the interesting things about low-fat and low-carb diets is that they sometimes make you realize what you really crave. If you wonder, you can always take the Baked Potato Test.

Why do you enjoy that baked potato so much? Is it the potato you love or the high-fat condiments you dollop on top?

You'd never eat three tablespoons of sour cream and butter on a plate by themselves. You might try to eat the potato with nothing on it, but it wouldn't be too tasty. It's the combination that makes a baked potato, with butter and sour cream, such a classic.

Now here's the test.

Think about replacing the sour cream and butter with something low-fat. Salsa is great on baked potatoes. Cottage cheese and chives are delicious on top. If your main attraction to the baked potato with butter and sour cream was the starchy carbs in the potato, you'll be happy to switch toppings. A low-fat diet will be very manageable for you.

But if you just can't seem to find a topping that does the trick . . . it may be that what you really miss is the butter and the sour cream. You may be more attached to the fat. Even if you wouldn't eat the butter and sour cream by themselves, the fat content may be harder for you to reduce than the carbs. No problem. Try a low-carb diet. You won't feel like you're missing a thing!

The illiterate of the 21st century will not be those who cannot read and write, but those who cannot learn, unlearn, and relearn.

– Alvin Toffler

CUTTING CALORIES THE EASY WAY

The elbow exercise

This exercise has been proven to help anyone lose weight: Push yourself back from the table. Forget about eating everything on your plate. Eat the right amount, then get up from the table. Don't keep grazing.

Eat for your health

Food keeps us alive. It provides our body with nutrition. It also soothes and alters emotions. How many calories would you save if you ate only for nutritional reasons, not emotional reasons?

Focus on eating

Don't multitask. Have you ever eaten an entire bag of chips or cookies because you opened the bag just as you turned on the TV? The hand-to-mouth movement becomes automatic and before you know it, you've gobbled down 2,000 calories instead of 200. Don't do that!

Eat before you shop

Everything looks good if you're hungry. Eating a little healthy snack just before you hit the grocery store will help you make choices with your brain instead of your stomach.

Stop power eating

All the food you eat on the go, while rushing somewhere or powering through it, deprives you of the emotional and tactile satisfaction food is supposed to have. You're creating a deficit. The odds of your body asking to be compensated with comfort food later have just gone through the roof. Take a little extra time to enjoy the food you eat and you won't set up the emotional need for a high-calorie payback later.

WHEN 100 CALORIES AREN'T WORTH 100 CALORIES

You can do a lot with 100 calories, but not all calories are the same. Sometimes it just isn't worth it. You can eat 100 empty calories or 100 calories of high nutritional value. Each of the items below are under 100 calories. Which do you think would be the healthier choices?

Light beer	95 calories
Low-carb chips	90 calories
Apple	80 calories
Sweet potato	95 calories

You must begin to think of yourself as the person you want to be.

– David Viscott

MIDLIFE WEIGHT WOES

Metabolism drops during midlife for both men and women. That means that if you do the same things that were keeping your weight stable before, you will gain weight during midlife. It's not pleasant and it's not fair, but it's true.

Evelyn Tribole, R.D., has come up with nine tips for handling midlife weight woes.[26] Put these into practice and you can keep yourself from gaining weight!

[26] women.msn.com/299242.armx at Lifetimetv.com (July 5, 2004).

1. Lift weights

Lifting weights two to three times a week is important. The 10 to 15% drop in your metabolism is largely due to decreased muscle mass. Working out increases your muscle mass, improves your circulation, and makes you burn more calories all day long.

2. Aerobic exercise

Cardiovascular exercise is crucial. It will reduce weight gain and improve your health. Walking, jogging, cycling, swimming, or attending an aerobics class four or five days a week will help keep you fit.

3. Eat a balanced diet

Lower metabolism means that you can eat the same amount of food you've always eaten and still gain weight. Reducing calories and increasing exercise is the best response.

4. Eat smaller meals

Our body requires fewer calories as we age. We function much better on numerous small meals than a few big ones. Five or six small meals a day is ideal.

5. Eat satisfying foods

The hormonal shifts in our body at midlife make it harder to feel full and easier to overeat. So your best bet is to eat what Tribole calls "high-satiety foods." These are filling foods such as chicken, eggs, turkey, fish, beans, and nuts, and high-fiber foods such as whole-grain cereals, beans, fruits, whole-grain crackers, and vegetables.

6. Eat more at lunch

It's controversial, but some experts still say that eating your bigger meal in the middle of the day does the most to prevent weight gain.

7. Reduce alcohol

Alcohol is a culprit in abdominal weight gain. If you're worried about your gut, try limiting yourself to no more than one drink per day.

8. Reduce your stress

Years of stress can actually disrupt your hormonal balance. When that happens, your body will gain weight. Stress can cause weight gain, just like overeating can. Find the relaxation techniques that work best for you and practice them on a daily basis. Exercise, meditation, writing in your journal, therapy, and warm conversations with friends are some of the most popular and effective choices.

9. Become an optimist

The good news is that, even if you never regain the metabolism you had at 20, your metabolism will stabilize after midlife.

HOW MUCH DID YOU EAT?

Do you *really* know the amount of food you eat? If you do, you're the exception. Most people underestimate their portion sizes by as much as 75%![27]

It's always a good idea to buy a digital scale and measure your food — especially at the beginning of a diet. Before long, you'll train yourself to recognize a three-ounce chicken breast or one tablespoon of oil.

When you're not near a scale, here are a few tips to help you guesstimate:

- The tip of your thumb = 1 teaspoon

BOOK REFERENCE

How well can you guesstimate calories? Do you know which has more calories: a pretzel or a bowl of olives? Ten peanuts or three graham crackers? *Dr. Shapiro's Picture Perfect Weight Loss* is the best book I've seen on this topic. I'll say more about it in the next chapter, when we talk about specific foods. But his Food Quiz for testing your calorie IQ is amazing. You can find it at www.amazon.com by searching for Howard M. Shapiro, *Dr. Shapiro's Picture Perfect Weight Loss* (Warner Books, 2003).

[27] "Twelve Weeks to a New You," my.webmd.com. (July 30, 2004).

- A ping pong ball = 1 ounce or 2 tablespoons
- A deck of cards = 3 ounces of cooked meat without the bone
- A handful of grain = 1 cup

Strength does not come from winning. Your struggles develop your strengths. When you go through hardships and decide not to surrender, THAT is strength.

– Arnold Schwarzenegger

WHAT TRIGGERS YOUR EATING?

Because it can alter our brain chemistry, food can soothe us and change our mood. Nursing and bottle feeding are deeply comforting to us when we are infants. As children, we are exposed to countless situations in which food is a treat or a reward. Food literally has the ability to cheer us up. If nothing else, it stops that nagging pain of hunger that growls in our stomach when we haven't had enough food!

There's nothing pathological in enjoying the comforting aspects of food. A diet that attempts to strip away the pleasure of eating with its lack of variety, dull presentation, or bland menus will never have many advocates. Our bodies are designed to help us recognize the pleasurable aromas, tastes, and textures of food. It's a natural, healthy part of the eating experience.

On the other hand, it's fairly common to use food badly. Cooking your favorite dish at the end of a long, hard day may be a very appropriate response to stress. But if that food is bad for you, then it can have negative repercussions.

Using comfort food to avoid emotional problems isn't useful either. It's counter-productive. Eating in that way is only a temporary diversion that actually prevents us from learning the coping skills we need to deal with emotional distress.

One way to get thin is to re-establish a purpose in life.

– Cyril Connolly

EMOTIONAL OVEREATING

Emotional overeating usually falls into four main categories.[28] Have you habitually used food to cope with things in these categories?

- **Socially**

  Overeating in a social situation, due to tension, anxiety, a desire to please at your own expense, or feelings of inadequacy.

- **Emotionally**

  Overeating as a reaction to feelings of boredom, depression, anger, loneliness, anxiety, or low-self-worth.

- **Situationally**

  Overeating unconsciously while watching TV, going to the movies, going to a sports event, or meeting with friends.

- **Physiologically**

  Overeating in response to physical cues, such as pain, headaches, or increased hunger after missing meals.

If you commonly fall prey to these emotional eating habits, the first step is to recognize the situations that trigger overeating for you. Then arm yourself with a game plan. Create two or three alternatives that you can substitute the next time the situation occurs.

BEGIN BY MAKING BETTER CHOICES

In terms of weight loss alone, you might begin by substituting healthier foods for the foods you're overeating in these situations. At a movie, popcorn without butter is a good substitute for high-fat, chemical-laden "buttered" popcorn. Keeping healthy snacks at work

---

[28] Grayson, M.D., Charlotte. "Emotional Eating," http://content.health.msn.com/content/article/48/ (August 2003).

or in your car will help you stave off the hunger pains that set you up for overeating later. In the next chapter, you'll find tips for some of my favorite snacks.

Substitution can help you meet your health and diet goals. But if you notice that you are frequently turning to food for emotional reasons, you may want to look for other ways to meet those emotional needs. Food is not doing it. It is merely prolonging the pain. Somewhere inside you know that, so it will ultimately make you feel frustrated and unhappy.

Therapy, meditation, massage, volunteer work, social activities, and any number of other solutions are better at meeting your emotional needs than a bag of chips or piece of pie. Don't cheat yourself. You deserve the best. Keep looking till you find what you really need.

DIET BLUNDER: EXPECTING TOO MUCH TOO SOON

This is the most common diet blunder. With all the fad diets promising that you can lose 10 pounds in a week or 30 pounds in a month, it's hard to avoid getting your hopes up!

The most healthy rate of weight loss is only about two pounds per week. But that feels slow. A lot of people set their goals much higher, then feel like they've failed when they lose a measly two pounds!

According to Paula Kennedy of WeightWatchers.com, the antidote is to make "slow and steady" your diet mantra. She suggests going to the grocery store and picking up a chunk of butter. That's right. A pack of fat. Pick up two pounds of it and hold it in your hands. Do you *still* think two pounds isn't very much?

CREATE A FOOD JOURNAL

You *can* find a diet that will change your life.

What you eat can make you healthier. It can improve your energy level. Instead of dragging through the day, you can make food choices that will help you sustain your energy all day long. Add a solid exercise program to that and you'll put so much spring in your step, you'll think you were 20 years younger!

If you do all that for two weeks or two months and then you stop, it's all over. No matter how great you feel on a well-balanced program of diet and exercise, you can quickly and easily revert to flab and sluggishness. There may be no easy way to lose weight, but there are *a lot of easy ways* to gain it back!

YOUR HUNGER'S IN YOUR HEAD
According to the National Institute of Health, it takes time for your brain to realize how much you've eaten. You feel hungry and you eat. The nerves in your upper digestive tract send a message to the hypothalamus in your brain to stop the hunger. But there's a time lag before the feeling of hunger goes away. If you eat too quickly, you can easily eat more than you need!

All this means is that it's crucial to find a diet and exercise program that suits you. The closer you can get to choosing a program that matches your lifestyle now, the better you'll be able to keep doing it in the long run.

The best way to choose a diet that's right for you is to start with a food journal. Most people eat without giving it much thought. It's harder to come up with a lifetime eating plan that will match your current patterns if you don't really know what those patterns are.

Do you tend to eat more carbs in the morning or the evening? How often, in a week, do you eat to alter a mood? How often does your mood determine the food you choose to eat? How many vegetables do you eat in a typical week? How many hours apart are your meals? How often are you hungry? Although each of these questions is important in identifying your eating patterns, many people are unable to answer them accurately.

By keeping a food journal for one week before you begin your diet, you will discover a lot of interesting things about what you eat, when you eat, and why you eat. All of those things will help you choose the diet that's best for you.

What to Include in the journal:

1. What you eat
2. What you drink
3. Portion sizes
4. Times you eat
5. The mood you're in just before you eat

Once you have kept your food journal for a week, look it over. Do you notice any patterns? How does your typical way of eating match up to the diet you're considering?

The tragedy in life doesn't lie in not reaching your goal.
The tragedy lies in having no goal to reach.

– Benjamin Mays

How to evaluate your patterns

Ask yourself these questions as you look at your journal. Begin each question with the phrase, "On a typical day . . ."

1. How many calories do you consume?
2. How many meals do you eat?
3. What do you enjoy eating most?
4. What would be hardest for you to give up?
5. What would you like to change about your eating pattern?

It is far better to change two or three things a week over time than to make a radical shift in your diet that doesn't last.

Keep in mind that fewer than 5% of dieters make permanent lifestyle changes. If you're really going to do this, you need to give yourself as many advantages as you can!

With so many diets out there, it's worthwhile to take your time in finding the right choice for you. Look for a plan that comes as close to your existing patterns as possible, while making the important changes that will get the results you need.

RESPECT YOUR BODY

Respect the fact that your body is a complex, organic system. Your mind can make a decision about a diet in seconds, but it's your body that's going to experience the adjustments. Give yourself a break. Select a diet that starts where you are and moves in a healthier, more effective direction.

If you love red meat and potatoes, don't expect your body to embrace an all-vegan diet overnight. If you always gravitate toward pasta, bread, and french fries, you're probably better off with a diet that cuts back on carbs rather than a high-protein diet that virtually eliminates carbs altogether.

Think about your own patterns. If you never cook, it's not a good idea to leap immediately into a food regimen that will require you to cook all of your meals every day. Keep it closer to your usual patterns. Find a way to buy most of the meals at first and gradually break into cooking. It's a big enough shift to change what you eat. Asking yourself to change too many things at once is asking for trouble.

Look for creative solutions that will make it easier for you to change your diet permanently from where it is now to where you want it to be. For instance, Trader Joe's has a lot of wonderful pre-cooked meals. Their flash-frozen fish and chicken can be turned into meals so quickly that it's almost like not cooking at all! Check out my website, too, at www.gethappy-gethealthy-bewealthy.com. One of the ways I get around cooking all week long is to make meals in big batches, then freeze them. I've included lots of recipes there for you to use.

A COOKIE CAN STOP YOUR BODY FROM BURNING FAT!

Sugary carbs like cookies flood your bloodstream with glucose (blood sugar). The sugar spike triggers an insulin response that turns *on* fat production and turns *off* fat burning!

Committing to a healthy diet is one of the best things you can do for yourself. It can literally add decades of good, vibrant years to your life. You owe it to yourself and the people you love to choose the healthiest diet possible.

When some people compare what they actually eat to what they know they *should be* eating, the idea of change seems overwhelming. But, as the old Chinese saying goes, "A journey of a thousand miles begins with a single step." If you're feeling overwhelmed, pick five things you'd like to change about your diet. Then change them, one thing at a time, for five weeks. You don't need enough willpower and determination to do it all right now. You only need enough to choose one right thing—today, then the next day, then the next. A little extra effort on your part, sustained over time, can take you where you want to go.

QUICK TIP
For more recipes and food tips, go to www.gethappy-gethealthy-bewealthy.com

What lies behind us and what lies before us are tiny matters compared to what lies within us.

– Ralph Waldo Emerson

CHAPTER 7

Choosing to Eat Healthy

To eat is a necessity, but to eat intelligently is an art.

– La Rochefoucauld

Dr. Barry Sears, author of *The Zone*, says, "Food is the most powerful drug you will ever take." He's absolutely right. Food is our "fuel." It order to keep our body running at its optimum capacity, we need to burn the highest quality fuel and know exactly what "octane" to use.

What do you eat? The fuel you put in your body is one of the best indicators of how healthy you will be. Would you like to improve your health? Are you beginning to notice a drop in your energy? Have your bones begun to ache? Is it a struggle to walk up a couple flights of stairs? Do you have to drag yourself out of bed in the mornings and drug yourself to sleep?

This chapter will help you change all that. A healthy body, fueled day after day with rich nutrients, doesn't suffer the same weakness or debilitating illness as a body that is forced to survive on inadequate nutrition for years at a time. There's a heavy toll to pay for neglecting your health.

By learning how to eat a more healthy diet, you can dramatically improve your vitality and literally add years to your life. I don't mean years of limping around on a walker, trying to remember your name, but vibrant, happy, healthy years. Nutrition is one of the most crucial keys to good health.

You can buy the best car in the world, but if you fill it up with corrosive, inadequate, low-octane fuel, it will run like a junker. Your body is even more precious. Its health is directly linked to your happiness, vitality, and longevity.

How many times do you eat every day? Every single time you put food in your mouth, you have an opportunity to improve your health.

Don't put this off. Get it right. Read this chapter carefully. Learn everything you can about the foods that can fight cancer, boost your immune system, reduce your cholesterol, and give you vibrant health. There's no need to start tomorrow. Start today—with the next piece of food you put in your mouth.

It's time to make the right choices. Your life depends on it.

Those who think they have no time for healthy eating
will sooner or later have to find time for illness.

– Edward Stanley

TRADER JOE'S: THE PERFECT ONE-STOP SHOP

I buy almost all of my food at Trader Joe's. I can't recommend it highly enough. Because you can do almost all of your shopping there, it is the perfect one-stop shop. I think of it as the "low-stress" answer to shopping and cooking. It is not only convenient, but it provides consistently high-quality products. Most of their food is organic and offers you the interesting diversity of gourmet selections. It allows you to easily stay on your food plan.

Go to my website at www.gethappy-gethealthy-bewealthy.com for numerous recipes using Trader Joe's products. They are very quick to cook and many recipes can be made ahead for added convenience!

The tremendous success of Trader Joe's has resulted in hundreds of stores opening all across the country. Find a location near you and see a list of their products at www.traderjoes.com. If you are near one of their locations, be sure to check it out. For healthy gourmet foods, wines, herbs, supplements, organic products, and other supplies, they can't be beat. Not only is their quality among the finest, but they have great low prices too!

HOW MUCH DO YOU KNOW ABOUT FOOD?

Most of the time, we know it when we blow it.

You're rushing between business meetings at 2:00 P.M. across town and you didn't pack a lunch. The place you usually go to grab a healthy salad or sandwich is out of your way. You pop into a shop that looks like a good alternative, but there's a line all the way to the door. So you pull up to the drive-in window at a fast food place.

The doctor of the future will give no medication,
but will interest his patients in the care of the human frame,
diet, and in the cause and prevention of disease.

– Thomas A Edison

Eating something is better than nothing, you tell yourself. If you don't eat, your metabolism is going to drop. Your blood sugar will plummet close behind it. Soon you won't be able to concentrate and the effort will be making you cranky. You don't have much time, but you can't afford to let all that stuff happen! So you make a choice.

You try to do the least damage by ordering a chicken sandwich without the mayo, but then you discover the questionable chicken filet they've given you is fried. You're starved. You're in a hurry. You eat it. Things happen. Life goes on.

It can happen to anybody. If you're committed to getting healthy and improving the quality of your life, those moments will be few and far between.

I'm much more concerned about the foods that *seem* like good choices, but aren't. Most of us think we have a pretty good idea about what we're eating, but it's not always the case.

Self-delusion is pulling in your stomach
when you step on the scales.

– Paul Sweeney

Dr. Howard Shapiro has written a book, *Dr. Shapiro's Picture Perfect Weight Loss,* that makes that vividly clear. The photos in his food demonstrations convey his point better than anything I've ever seen. He asks, "How much do you really know about making healthy food choices?" Then he offers a food quiz to test your knowledge. I highly recommend it.

To get a sampling of the kind of brain teasers you'll be up against in that quiz, I'll mention a few here. All of us know that a slab of chocolate cake has more calories than an apple. That's a no-brainer. But life isn't as easy as that. Neither is Dr. Shapiro's quiz.

Which of the following is *lower* in calories?

- English muffin with jam or dry bagel?
- Turkey on rye or peanut butter and jelly on whole wheat?

Some of you have choked down that dry bagel instead of luxuriating in a crispy English muffin with your favorite jam, thinking you were being healthy—maybe even cutting back on calories. If that's what you thought, you were wrong. According to Dr. Shapiro, an English muffin with jam is only 170 calories. The dry bagel? A whopping 400.

VIDEO ONLINE: YOUR FOOD—10 YEARS FROM NOW

What you're eating now can make or break your health 10 years from now. Find out how in a streaming video online. It's an ABC Special Report: abcnews.go.com/sections/GMA/HealthyWoman/GMA020820Weight_10years.html.

And how about the turkey on rye? That's got to be the lower calorie choice, right? Peanut butter is high fat, jelly is sweet . . . If you chose the rye, you're wrong again. It's 410 calories, but the peanut butter and jelly on whole wheat comes in at 365.

To take the full quiz, order *Dr. Shapiro's Picture Perfect Weight Loss* (Warner Books, 2003). It's filled with food comparisons that will surprise you.

PUTTING TOGETHER A HEALTHY MEAL

The key to a healthy meal is a combination of foods that provides you a balance of nutrients. Be sure to include:

- **Protein**

  Lean meats, eggs, fish, nuts, seeds, and beans are excellent choices. Protein is vital for rebuilding and maintaining your body tissues.

- **Starchy carbohydrates**

  Whole grains in bread, pasta, pitas, and crackers are starchy carbs. Brown rice, quinoa, barley, couscous, corn, potatoes, sweet potatoes, and yams are great choices too. Carbs provide your body with a readily available source of energy. They also hold the key to converting food into fuel by providing the vitamins you need for that process.

- **Fruits and vegetables**

  Low in calories, these foods are rich in vitamins and minerals. For the vital dark, leafy greens, choose Romaine lettuce, spinach, kale, collard greens, mustard greens, dandelion greens, watercress, arugula, mesclun, bok choy, and Swiss chard (red and yellow). Don't forget carrots, zucchini, sprouts, onions, leeks, radishes, tomatoes, bell peppers, and squash. Always pick fresh fruit over canned or frozen. And always choose fruit over juice, which contains little or no fiber and often raises your blood sugar too quickly.

EAT THE RAINBOW

Not only do the colors in fruits and vegetables reflect different vitamin and mineral content, but they give you added protection! The rich colors protect the plants against sun damage and disease. They can do the same for you. Eat lots of dark leafy greens, bright oranges, sunny yellows, brilliant reds, beautiful purples. Look for kale, spinach, prunes, raisins, cherries, and squash in your diet. Don't forget that potatoes alone come in several colors—white, brown, red, yellow, and purple. Be sure to include a rainbow of color in your diet every day!

When diet is wrong medicine is of no use.
When diet is correct medicine is of no need.

– Ancient Ayurvedic proverb

INTERACTIVE HEALTHY EATING INDEX

The USDA Center for Nutrition Policy and Promotion has one of the hottest online nutrient calculators around. And it's *free!*

This year, they've added a new component called the physical activity tool. It not only assesses your physical activity status, but it provides you with energy expenditure calculations. Together, these tools help you guarantee that you're getting the benefit of good nutrition and regular physical activity.

Check out the Interactive Healthy Eating Index at http://www.usda.gov/cnpp or go directly to that link at http://209.48.219.53.

PORTABLE BREAKFASTS

Oatmeal is truly a wonder food that most people don't cook properly. When it comes out like glop or wallpaper paste, you're not going to be too interested in eating it! If you cook it right and add some special touches—for extra flavor, color, and nutritional value—you can make oatmeal a satisfying meal. Instead of cringing at a clump of white paste in your bowl, you'll look forward to starting your day with this delicious, healthy food.

I have tried all of the brands and can recommend the best of rolled, steel cut, regular oatmeal and "instant oatmeal" for travel. It's great with lots of fruit and nuts. (See my website at www.gethappy-gethealthy-bewealthy.com for recipes.) When you're too busy to stop for breakfast, oatmeal makes a great portable meal too. I simply make it thinner and drink it out of an insulated mug.

THE WORLD'S HEALTHIEST FOODS

Another great source of information about the nutritional value of food is a website called The World's Healthiest Foods. You can find it at www.whfoods.com. They have quick and healthy recipes too!

Muesli is another great alternative. If I have to leave very early the next morning, I often mix up a large cup of muesli before I go to bed. It's perfect when I plan to be flying early in the morning. I make it the night before, so I can just grab it and go. I eat/drink it on the way to the airport.

Cookies are extremely convenient and portable. The same nuts, fruits, oats, and grains you would eat in a bowl for breakfast can easily be turned into cookies. I make very nutritious cookies out of oatmeal, protein powder, fruit, and nuts for an easy-to-carry, nutritious alternative. You can find some of my favorites on the website.

KITCHEN APPLIANCES THAT HELP YOU EAT HEALTHY FOOD

George Foreman's grill

You don't need to be a boxing fan to love the George Foreman grill. It's the best on the market. There are other grills out there, but this one is easy, convenient, and affordable. You'll find it online at www.amazon.com. or at any kitchen supply store.

FoodSaver vacuum packaging system

To make your food last five times longer than usual, try the remarkable FoodSaver. It is the leading vacuum packaging system in the country. Tightly sealing your food is a great healthy alternative that will save you time and money, while keeping your food fresh.

SmartPot crock pot

The SmartPot is one of my favorite ways to cook. It allows me to make a large quantity of food at one time with very little fuss. Then I use the FoodSaver to package and freeze it for when I don't have time to cook.

If you thought they couldn't improve the crock pot, think again! Now it comes with a programmable timer. All you do is preset the time and temperature, then go about your day. The new "smart pot" will automatically switch on to have your meal ready in time. When it is finished cooking, it will reduce itself to the warm setting to keep your meal ready.

That means less stressful meals and less time cooking! It's healthy and economical too. The crock pot allows you to use less expensive cuts of meat, since they get really tender when they are cooked so slowly. I use it whenever I know I'm going to be late getting home.

You can get it ready first thing in the morning, but I make the process even easier on myself. I put all of the ingredients in the night before, then stick the removable pot in the refrigerator overnight. In the morning, I just take it out, plug it in, and set the timer.

The recipes are preloaded in the SmartPot's computer, so it is very easy. I like to make large amounts each time, so I can use the leftovers for healthy, fast lunches.

For ordering information and more recipes, check out www.rivco.com or any kitchen shop. See my website, www.gethappy-gethealthy-bewealthy.com, for recipes to use in your crock pot.

The discovery of a new dish does more for human happiness than the discovery of a new star.

– Jean Anthelme Brillat-Savarin

PANCAKES AND MUFFINS ENDORSED BY THE AMERICAN HEART ASSOCIATION?

Bruce's Sweet Potato Pancake Mix makes this claim. I add a few tablespoons of baked sweet potato to the mix to make it even more nutritious. Try using pureed, ripe fruit as a topping and Benecol instead of butter. It makes a very healthy pancake or muffin. Adding raisins and pecans will add more flavor and nutritional value. Go to www.brucefoods.com for more information and family fitness ideas.

FOOD AND MOOD

Do you notice you feel happier after eating chocolate? Do you wish you knew a food that could boost your energy?

Elizabeth Somer and Jeanette Williams, authors of *The Food & Mood Cookbook,* offer good advice about some of the ways food affects your state of mind.

What's the power food?

Protein. If you need a quick "power lunch," try three ounces of lean protein plus vegetables and a whole-grain cracker. Dry-roasted nuts will work too, if you're on the run. My favorite power food is the unsalted, dry roasted almonds from Trader Joe's. They have no sodium, provide lots of fiber, and are very tasty. Almonds help protect against prostrate cancer, so that is one more reason for men to consider them.

High-protein food increases the tyrosine in your blood—which forms the neurotransmitters, dopamine, and norephinephrine—and improves your concentration and alertness.

What food reduces anxiety?

Fat. Eating wild salmon, sardines, or tuna several times a week will provide your body with the omega-3 oils it needs. Reducing the saturated fats in your diet will help too.

What drink perks you up?

Coffee, of course. But did you know that green tea works too? Green tea has less caffeine than black tea and more antioxidants. It also has an animo acid called L-theanine, which creates alert relaxation.

What food works like Prozac?

Carbohydrates. They increase the levels of serotonin in your brain. Processed carbs and high-sugar carbs can create a backlash by raising your blood sugar level quickly, then letting it plummet again. You're better off with whole grains and starchy vegetables. Be sure to combine them with protein, fat, and fiber. Too many carbs at one time can make you sleepy!

The more you know about food, the more accurately you can make good food choices. Eating healthy begins with knowing what to eat—and why!

Eat what you like and let the food fight it out in your belly.

– Mark Twain

HOW FAST IS YOUR METABOLISM TODAY?

How quickly your body processes the food you eat depends on your metabolism. We all know that everyone's metabolism is different. Not only that, but *your* metabolism is different all the time. If you walked briskly for 30 minutes four days last week, but only two days this week, your metabolism was probably higher last week than it is now.

But how can you know for sure?

If only someone could calculate exactly how much weight you lost this week and measure it against what you ate and how much exercise you got, they could tell you exactly how many calories you burn in a week. They could tell you exactly how your metabolism was different last week than this week and how long it will take you to reach your goals.

DietPower does exactly that.

Keep track of the food you eat by logging it into the DietPower software. DietPower will tell you its nutritional content and its ratio of protein to carbohydrate to fat. It will chart your progress toward your goal and tell you exactly how fast your metabolism is running.

No other calorie counter monitors your metabolism to guarantee reaching your goal. You can add your own foods to the database or use the 11,000 foods provided. It analyzes 33 nutrients from recipes, counts the calories you burned through exercise, monitors your water intake, and gives you personalized advice. For a free trial, go to www.dietpower.com.

You are what you eat.

– American proverb

EXCHANGE GOOD FAT FOR BAD FAT

One of the best ways to eat healthy is to exchange "good" fat for "bad" fat.

Not all fats are bad. Our bodies need good fats (monounsaturated fats, like those in nuts, avocados, seeds, and olives) to keep our skin and joints properly lubed! It's the bad fats (saturated fats, such as butter and animal fat) that clog our arteries and pile the pounds on our thighs.

With a few substitutions, you can eliminate saturated fats painlessly!

Breakfast food:	Buttered toast
Substitute:	Almond butter on toast
Lunch food:	Tacos with cheddar cheese on top
Substitute:	Tacos with avocado on top
Snack food:	A bag of potato chips
Substitute:	A handful of nuts
Dinner food:	Pasta with alfredo sauce
Substitute:	Pasta with pesto sauce

BOOST YOUR FIBER

Leslie Bonci, R.D., author of *The ADA Guide to Better Digestion*, reminds us that fiber keeps our digestive system working, binds cholesterol so it doesn't get stuck in our arteries, and slows down glucose absorption. Here are five great foods filled with fiber:

Black beans	15 grams per cup	227 calories
Potatoes	10 grams per cup	160 calories
Acorn squash	10 grams per cup	114 calories
Barley	6 grams per cup	193 calories
Raspberries	8 grams per cup	60 calories

ANTIOXIDANTS IN A CAN

Fresh food is far and away your best choice for produce. But the demands of our busy schedules mean that compromises sometimes have to be made. If you got to compromise, here's a great way to do it: Eat canned corn.

Researchers at Cornell have found that canned corn actually has *more* antioxidants than fresh corn!

The canning process heats the corn to 239 degrees for 25 minutes. The result? Canned corn has more than 500 times the antioxidants than fresh corn.

What is food to one man may be poison to others.

– Lucretius

READ THE LABEL!

The labels on canned and packaged foods can help you make healthy choices. Keep in mind that the packagers who are trying too hard to sell their products do not always have your best interests in mind! The FDA keeps a close watch on their representations. Would a packager from a food company deliberately mislead you about the calories, fat, or sugar content of their products? You bet.

This means you need to become a savvy consumer. To eat a healthy diet, you have to learn to recognize what the food nutrition labels are *really* saying. Packaging is the food industry equivalent of political spin. You can't always take it at face value.

Here are four things to check:

1. Calories

Calories are often matched to tiny serving sizes. The calories in a single "serving" of soda may represent half a can of soda or less. Compare the amount in a serving to the actual ounces in the product. (And get your calculator ready. You're going to need it!)

2. **Serving size**

   Many products claim to be low-cal because they have reduced the serving size. Check the label. The company may be claiming that the small bag of pretzels you're eating is three servings!

3. **Sodium content**

   This is especially important when you buy frozen food. Those wonderful, pre-cut, convenient bags of frozen broccoli can have literally thousands of grams of sodium. Frozen dinners are even worse. Are you really willing to trade a quick-and-easy meal for bloating?

4. **Sugars**

   Watch out for the sugar content on supposedly healthy juice drinks. A lot of juice companies add so many sugars that you might as well be eating a donut!

> *It used to be standard practice that the pre-match meal consisted of egg, steak, and chicken. But I talked them into changing to complex carbohydrates. So now they will sup on porridge, pasta, or rice.*
>
> – Craig Johnston, Liverpool Football Club, 1989

HAVE YOU HEARD THE LATEST?

As residents of the Information Age, we are virtually compelled to keep up with the latest information as much as we can. Science has made great strides in nutrition in the last 10 years. Some of the things you've always been told may not be true anymore!

Knowledge is power. The more you know about how to eat well, the more

QUICK TIP
Omega-3 oils can improve your health and your mood, lower your risk of heart disease, and soften your skin. Salmon, tuna, trout, and mackerel have high concentrations of omega-3. Eat up!

effectively you can guarantee your longevity and vibrant health.

One of the best sources of up-to-date information is The Wellness Letter of the University of California, Berkeley. These facts are from a recent update:

WEB REFERENCE
How much fiber are you eating every day? Check it out for yourself at the U.S. Department of Agriculture's Nutrient Data Laboratory at www.nal.usda.gov/fnic.

- **It's OK to eat eggs.**

Old news: Eggs have 215 milligrams of cholesterol. So they should be bad for you.

The latest: It's saturated fats that raise cholesterol in the blood. Eggs have very little.

DELICIOUS EGG SUBSTITUTES

Since many guidelines still limit you to one egg a day, I use egg substitutes on a very regular basis, especially when larger quantities of eggs are needed.

Trader Joe's carries a brand called NULAID which works really well, as do all of the regular brands. I use it in cooking, baking, and everything that calls for eggs. One of my favorite ways to use it is in healthy, crust-less quiches.

Omelets are very light and fluffy with NULAID. I've found that two of the best omelets by far are made with NULAID and a combination of parmesan and prosciutto or spinach and kalamata olives. The recipes are on my website. Check out all my recipes with egg substitutes at www.gethappy-gethealthy-bewealthy.com.

He that takes medicine and neglects diet
wastes the skill of the physician.

– Chinese proverb

- **Popcorn is nutritious.**

  Old news: Whole wheat is better for you than corn. Popcorn is junk food.

  The latest: Corn is a whole grain, just like wheat. Popcorn has the same nutrients as the corn kernels it was made from.

- **Colored food is better.**

  Old news: Colors are unrelated to nutrition.

  The latest: Deeply colored fruits and vegetables have the most vitamins and minerals.

- **Salt doesn't cause high blood pressure.**

  Old news: Salt is related to high blood pressure.

  The latest: High salt intake can make high blood pressure worse in people who are sensitive to it. Try to keep your salt intake below 2,400 milligrams a day.

- **Chocolate is good for you.**

  Old news: Chocolate is bad for you.

  The latest: Chocolate has the same beneficial antioxidants as tea. One ounce of dark chocolate is the antioxidant equivalent of a cup of black tea.

HIGH-QUALITY FOODS TO ADD TO YOUR DIET

Eating a good balance of protein, starchy carbohydrates, fruits, and vegetables is the foundation of improving your health. With that foundation in place, you can start to add significant improvements.

These are a few of my favorites. Not only do they add flavor and enjoyment to my day, but they work for me actively to stave off disease, reduce my cholesterol, and slow aging, among many other things. They're easy enough to add to your life. Why not start today?

Drinking green tea

I look forward to drinking my green tea in the morning, It's soothing, yet it also helps to wake me up in the morning and makes me more alert.

Although we now have thousands of varieties of tea in the world, they fall into three main categories: black, oolong, and green tea.

Green tea is unique because it is not fermented. This gives tremendous health benefits that the others don't have. With black and oolong teas, the powerful antioxidants in tea are lost in the fermenting process. Green tea retains its antioxidant benefits.

It also contains powerful polyphenols such as tannins, catchins, and flavenoids, along with many other vitamins and minerals. It is especially high in vitamin C.

Green Tea Benefits, which sells green tea exclusively, cites some of these advantages of drinking green tea.

- Boosts your immune system
- Lowers blood sugar
- Slows the aging process
- Lowers cholesterol
- Burns calories
- Reduces blood pressure
- Protects against arthritis
- Reduces the risk of stroke and heart disease

For further information about the benefits of green tea, go to www.green-tea-benefits.com. There you will find an interesting history of green tea and dozens of varieties to order online.

I wasn't feeling well in the first half. Then I had three slices of pizza . . . and the food took me down.

– Leroy Loggins, basketballer with the Brisbane Bullets, after 1986 semi-final

Why I eat golden flaxseed every day

Flaxseeds are one of the best things you can put in your stomach. Some nutritionists believe that, after multivitamins, flaxseed may be the single most important supplement available.

Many health food stores sell the oil (which must be refrigerated) and several varieties of the seeds, organic and non-organic. Always buy organic, if you can. And get the golden seeds, rather than brown. They are much higher in healthy qualities, taste better, and digest much more easily. I eat one-eighth of a cup twice a day. The seeds are high in omega-3 oils.

Before you eat them, the shells need to be broken. I grind no more that two days' worth at a time, then keep them refrigerated so they stay fresh. (Do not freeze them, since that will eliminate some of the oil.)

The best grinder I've found is the Bosch grinder from Trader Joe's.

Here are just a few of the benefits of flaxseed:

- Lowers cholesterol
- Lowers triglycerides
- Prevents blood clots in arteries
- Protects against high blood pressure, inflammation, water retention
- Improves immune function
- Reduces recovery time in fatigued muscles after working out
- Increases energy and stamina
- Accelerates healing of sprains and bruises
- Improves absorption of calcium
- Improves eyesight
- Improves liver function
- Relieves symptoms of rheumatoid arthritis
- Alleviates some allergies
- Remedies some cases of depression
- Improves mental function in the aged
- Relieves some cases of PMS

For further information, check out these websites:

- ga.essortment.com
- www.flaxgold.com
- www.heintzmanfarms.com (At this site, you can order a free sample, along with information on how flaxseeds can help prevent diabetes.)

Three foods you may not eat often enough

If you're like most people, you probably aren't getting enough of three important foods: cranberries, almonds, and orange peel.

Cranberries have long been known for their ability to treat and prevent urinary tract infections. But they have other benefits as well. They can help prevent kidney stones, lower LDL and raise HDL (good) cholesterol, aid in recovery from stroke, and reduce the risk of getting cancer.

Almonds can also lower your risk of heart disease, due to their high concentration of vitamin E. Almonds' monounsaturated fats can lower LDL cholesterol by 8 to 12%. They are also high in the important minerals magnesium and potassium.

Orange peel contains a host of phytonutrients not as readily available in other foods. These nutrients lower both blood pressure and cholesterol. They also have strong anti-inflammatory properties. Practitioners of ancient Chinese herbal medicine have been putting orange peels in their remedies for over 3,000 years, knowing that the greatest healing properties were in the peel, not the liquid orange center.

These foods are so important that I make sure to include them in my diet on a regular basis. I make cookies with Trader Joe's whole organic oats, cranberries, almonds, orange peel, and protein powder with no sugar added. They're very nutritious and good tasting. Great for healthy snacks and quick breakfasts! The recipe is on my website at www.gethappy-gethealthy-bewealthy.com. I also use all three as additions to oatmeal and salads for color, taste, and crunch.

HEALTHY PIES AND FRUIT TARTS

Sound too good to be true? Normally, pie crust is notoriously high in saturated fat, because of added shortening or lard. I make wonderful, healthy crusts, using either canola, light olive, or Enova oil. You can too. Choose whole wheat flour for a nutty taste, then replace your portions of saturated fat with a healthy, unsaturated alternative. It's equally delicious and much better for you.

If you puree very ripe fruit and add it to the whole fruit, you'll need little or no sugar for the filling. Try adding low-fat ricotta cheese or yogurt to the filling for added protein and flavor. A slice of pie will give you at least one daily serving of fruit, sometimes more.

TRADER JOE'S TIP: OCUMARE

Now that dark chocolate has been proven to be beneficial in moderation, I can recommend my favorite chocolate: Ocumare. This Trader Joe's chocolate from Venezuela is for chocolate connoisseurs. It is 71% cocoa and has only three grams of sugar. One square makes a rich, delicious dessert.

WANT A 35-CALORIE DESSERT?

Along with Trader Joe's Venezuelan chocolate, I also eat rich "After Eight" mints as a dessert. If you eat one slowly, you will get the full sensation of a chocolate mint dessert for 35 calories (and only 8 carbs!).

On alternate nights, I eat a square of very dark chocolate (never milk chocolate). It is filled with healthy antioxidants. It raises the endorphins in your brain. And it's delicious.

WHERE TO FIND HEALTHY RECIPES

The Internet is a constant source of healthy recipes. Here are a few of the best sites for recipes. There is never any reason to eat the same ol' thing again!

www.cookinglight.com

www.foodfit.com

www.aicr.org (American Institute for Cancer Research)

www.deliciousdecisions.org (American Heart Association)

www.foodwatch.com.au

With the Internet, there's no need for a recipe box of crinkled, splattered 3 × 5 cards anymore. Simply bookmark your favorites on any given site or save your favorites to a handy recipe software program.

The Cookbook Wizard recipe software is an excellent program that was named ZDNET's Editors Pick. You can download a free trial copy at www.mealmaster.com.

Pocket Cook has won Best Software awards for two years running. It can be downloaded onto your PDA and taken to the grocery store with you! It makes printing out shopping lists obsolete. For a free trial copy, go to www.pocketcook.net.

PRIZE-WINNING CHICKEN POT PIE

A few years ago, I entered the Telegram-Tribune contest in San Luis Obispo County. I'd won several bake-offs at my wife's church, so I thought my chicken pot pie might stand a chance. To my surprise, it won first place!

Most pot pies are heavy and taste like crust. This one is full of fresh, local produce. It's light and very flavorful. People have been asking me for the recipe ever since I won. It's one of my favorites too. I hope you'll enjoy it. You can find this and more of my award-winning recipes on my website: www.gethappy-gethealthy-bewealthy.com.

MORE RECIPES ON MY WEBSITE

As my wife will tell you, I'm always experimenting in the kitchen. As I come up with new, healthy recipes that win rave reviews from my unsuspecting taste testers (my family and friends), I'll post them on my site. Check back regularly for new food tips and recipes at www.gethappy-gethealthy-bewealthy.com.

NO NEED FOR SACRIFICE

With so many choices of healthy foods to choose from, there's no need to sacrifice flavor and enjoyment. In case you don't already know it, the best, most succulent, mouth-wateringly delicious food is the freshest and most natural.

Have you ever bit into a fresh, ripe pear? Do you remember the taste of your first strawberry? Is there anything better than a hot sip of thick, hearty soup on a cold, wintry day?

Most of us know that healthy foods are not only better for us, but they often taste better and feel more satisfying as well. Years from now, when researchers look back on these years of poor diet and obesity in America, they may find that part of the trouble was our busy lives. We grab a candy bar or another cup of coffee because we tell ourselves we "don't have time to eat." We choke down a high-fat hamburger or some other fast-food nightmare because we're on the run and we didn't have time to prepare. Then, before we know it, we've gained 20 pounds and we're getting aches and pains from poor nutrition!

A healthy diet isn't an option. It's what it takes to live a long, enjoyable life.

But there's a limit.

Some people claim that a diet of 100% raw vegetables can make you live to be 150. So you have to ask yourself: Even if that were true, would it be worth it?

Maybe not. The secret to choosing a healthy diet for good—without rushing back to your old, unhealthy habits every other week—is to choose a diet that suits you. Don't eliminate things that add to your quality of life or soothe you emotionally. Those changes will be short-lived. You need to do better than that.

Our lives are not in the lap of our gods,
but in the lap of our cooks.

– Lin Yutang

Find ways to keep as many of the things you love in your life as possible. Just keep them in perspective. Even bodybuilders, on the most rigorous diet regimens, build in a "cheat meal" every week, where they indulge their sweet tooth, chow down a bag of potato chips, or have a beer. Every time they do it, they increase the odds of sticking with their diet. Moderation is the key.

NEED A QUICK SNACK?
My three favorites are Trader Joe's roasted, unsalted almonds; apples; and organic, low-fat yogurt. They're great for keeping your energy up throughout the day.

What I am saying is, you don't really have to give anything up! Do you love chocolate? Have a Trader Joe's Ocumare square. Are you craving something soft and creamy? Nothing's better than a bowl of blackberries with low-fat whipped cream—nutritious and amazingly low on calories. Do you miss those big, juicy steaks you used to eat in front of the TV every night? Have a smaller one as a treat, once a week.

Look for creative ways to hang onto foods that you really enjoy, while making sure they contribute to your crucial goal of good health. With so many delicious choices out there, you'll soon discover that healthy food makes eating an even greater pleasure than before.

The wise man should consider that health is the greatest of human blessings. Let food be your medicine.

– Hippocrates

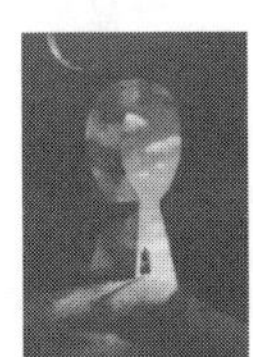

CHAPTER 8

Choosing to Exercise

Many people treat their bodies as if they were rented from Hertz—something they are using to get around in but nothing they genuinely care about understanding.

– Chungliang Al Huang

- You *can* lose that spare tire around your waist.
- You *can* look and feel 10 years younger.
- You *can* completely transform your body, once and for all.

How can I say this with such complete confidence? How do I know for sure? Because I've done it myself. With determination and hard work, I made remarkable changes in my own body. So I know that if I can do it, you can too!

A spare tire can creep up on you. If you eat just 500 extra calories a day, you can put on a spare tire easily in a couple of months. An order of fries, a frozen mocha, or a slice of pizza will give you close to 500 calories. If you super-size those fries, you can get there even faster!

As you can see from the "before" photos posted on my website (www.gethappy-gethealthy-bewealthy.com), I wasn't a couch potato. I was leading a fairly active life. When the first photo was taken, I was going snorkeling. But it's not a pretty picture. I'm not 53 in this photo. I'm barely 40. That's where it starts. A spare tire.

I noticed it and I didn't like it. But I didn't do anything significant about it. Maybe I cut back on fries or ate a salad for lunch now and then. Other guys my age were starting to get a gut too. We all made jokes about it. None of us took it seriously. So the months sped by. Four years later, as you can see, I was still wearing that spare. (And I'm sucking it in!)

With every month that passed, that spare tire got a little bigger and a little bigger, till one day I knew something had to change.

Make sure the outside of you is a good reflection of the inside of you.

– Jim Rohn

FROM FAT BOY TO MALE STRIPPER

When I decided to completely change my physique, my family and friends were supportive. They were *so* supportive, in fact, that I knew they would never hold me accountable—even if I failed. They'd love me no matter what. I was lucky to have that kind of support. But I knew I had to be harder on myself than that.

I could not allow myself to fail.

My greatest motivator was fear of public humiliation. Knowing that, I decided to set my goal high and tell everyone what it was. That way, there would be no going back. I'd be forced to succeed. So I did the only logical thing . . .

I entered a bodybuilding contest!

Of course, I knew absolutely nothing about bodybuilding. All I really knew was that bodybuilders were the epitome of fitness. They had state-of-the-art expertise on losing weight and getting in shape. That's what I wanted too.

As it turned out, I had a lot to learn. I read everything I could on bodybuilding and talked to experienced people at the gym. I quickly learned that a lot of bodybuilders take steroids, human growth hormone, blood enhancers, and other drugs or supplements to help them bulk up and lose fat. I wanted nothing to do with any of that.

I definitely wanted to look great, but not at the expense of my health! What's the point of looking great and dying young?

So I looked for a drug-free, natural approach. And I quickly found the answer. The good news is, it works great. And it'll work for you too. The bad news is, you're not going to like it. What's the best way to get in fantastic shape, drug-free? *Hard work!*

Everybody wants to know what I'm on. What am I on?
I'm on my bike busting my ass six hours a day. What are you on?

– Lance Armstrong, six-time
Tour de France winner, Nike ad 2000

Once I started working out, I earned the reputation of being the hardest-working guy at the gym. I was burning up calories fast, and I literally consumed my body weight in whey protein to put on muscle tissue. This was my program:

Get up at 4:30 A.M. (Since I was working 50+ hours a week, there was literally no time available to work out every day. So I cut back on sleep. And guess what? I never missed it.)

Three days a week: Circuit training-75 minutes to total muscle fatigue and exhaustion.

Three days a week: Cardio workouts on the off days (with one day of rest. Rest is a crucial component of a fitness program. It's in the resting period, not the working out period, that your body builds muscle.)

This was my schedule every week for a year, while I was training for the bodybuilding competition. It was so effective that I continue to keep this schedule today. During that year, I saw some incredible changes to my body—things I never thought I'd see in my physique. My chest filled out. My arms took on a new definition. I lost my spare tire and even developed abs!

But I underestimated the competition. Even though I'd been entering triathlons for 20 years and knew a thing or two about athletic contests, I was new to bodybuilding. I was up against guys who had been refining their program for years. So I didn't make the cut.

But I did make the tryouts!

The personal satisfaction that I achieved was extremely rewarding and all of the work was more than worthwhile. The biggest payoff was the fact that, at age 53, I looked the best I had looked in my whole life!

Check out the photos on my website (www.gethappy-gethealthy-bewealthy.com) and see for yourself. What do you think? Did I succeed?

The biggest problem we face in America is not terrorism.
The biggest problem we're facing in America is obesity.

– Dr. Julie Gerberding, Centers for
Disease Control and Prevention

THE REAL REWARD

At the end of that year, I was happy with the results of my hard work. I had lost over seven inches in my waist. Things were looking good. But that was just on the outside! What's more important is what happened on the inside.

- I started at 23% body fat and got down to a little over 10% body fat.
- My blood pressure dropped to 102/58.
- My resting heart rate dropped to 56.
- My cholesterol levels were down significantly and the ratios were good.

EXPLODING EXERCISE MYTHS

The Nutrition Action Newsletter is a wonderful source of health and fitness information. Check out their article on exercise myths! You'll be amazed at how many things that you've heard about exercise are wrong! www.cspinet.org/nah/2_00/ten_myths01.html.

WHAT WAS THE MORE IMPORTANT THING I LEARNED?

That everything in life is a choice. In order to change my body, here are a few of the things I chose:

- I chose to exercise six days a week.
- I chose to get up at 4:30 A.M. to make time for exercise.
- I chose what I put in my mouth.
- I chose my attitude.
- I chose success.

So here's my challenge to you. If you want it, make it happen. It's your choice.

If you want to change your body, you can do it. Learn as much as you can about it. Make a plan. Then work the plan. Every day. And you will change your body.

I did it. I challenge you to do the same.

Living a healthy lifestyle will only deprive you
of poor health, lethargy, and fat.

– Jill Johnson

CAN YOU REALLY LOSE 100 POUNDS WITHOUT SURGERY?

Absolutely. Here are three great websites, for men and women, filled with testimonials and amazing before-and-after photos from people who have lost enormous amounts of weight!

- **Men's Health Belly Off Club**

Go immediately to www.menshealth.com and check out their Men's Health Belly Off Club. Their fitness articles are excellent too.

- **Oprah Winfrey**

Be sure to visit Oprah Winfrey's website: www.oprah.com. There are lots of testimonials and very inspiring stories of weight loss success.

Bob Greene

Oprah's renowned trainer, Bob Greene, has a fantastic website of his own. You can find it at www.getwiththeprogram.org. Not only are the photographs incredible, but he has a highly successful program that starts with a very powerful tool—making a contract with yourself to get in shape.

This contract is one of the best ideas for fitness goals that I've come across. My approach to bodybuilding was very similar. By choosing to get ready for the bodybuilding contest, I made a contract with myself, in effect, to get in shape by that entry date. My results speak for themselves. With a contract, you make a firm commitment to yourself. It really helps.

If you have any doubt that you can do it, check out these great websites. There's nothing as inspiring as success!

GETTING STARTED

Getting started is probably the hardest thing about changing your body. Once you add exercise to your schedule and start feeling the benefits, it's much easier to keep going.

It helps to think of your body like an engine. Your body needs fuel (calories). You have the choice of burning fuel in a way that makes your body stronger and more powerful or keeps you idling at a pitiful, couch potato pace.

What you want more of is muscle—even if it's not your goal to be a bodybuilder. Here's why. Muscle burns 18 times more calories than fat. Doing nothing, your body burns calories. It burns 18 times more calories for every ounce of muscle than it does for every ounce of fat. Why not take advantage of this? If you add more muscle, you will boost your metabolism and get rid of excess calories faster.

When you add exercise to your life every day, the changes you'll see in your body will astound you. And the beauty of exercise is that it usually makes you feel a lot better right away. The endorphin rush you feel after 30 minutes or more of vigorous exercise will keep you coming back again and again.

Many of the health benefits of exercise kick in much more quickly than other things you do to improve your health. Add an extra serving of fruits or vegetables to your diet and you'll be glad about eating right, but you may not feel an immediate difference. Taking a multivitamin is a good idea, but it isn't likely to make you run up a flight of stairs any faster. Exercise, on the other hand, will do exactly that!

It's not uncommon to feel energized from your first aerobic workout through your last. On the very first night after you work out, you're almost certain to sleep more soundly. One bout of vigorous exercise does so much for your circulation that you'll feel an immediate boost. You can't say that about many things that are good for you—but exercise is one of them.

We sit at breakfast, we sit on the train on the way to work,
we sit at work, we sit at lunch, we sit all afternoon,
a hodgepodge of sagging livers, sinking gallbladders,
drooping stomachs, compressed intestines, and squashed organs.

– John Button, Jr.

WHY DIDN'T GRANDPA WORK OUT?

Our ancestors didn't work out. (Health clubs were few and far between.) In fact, a lot of them ate meat and potatoes with gravy and an extra helping of butter! So why didn't they gain weight?

Researchers at the University of Tennessee studied the Amish community in Ontario to find the answer. This farming community lives a lot like our ancestors did 150 years ago. The women cook and clean without the benefit of electricity. The men tend the animals and plant the fields without modern equipment.

On an average week, researchers found that most of the Amish men in this community took about 18,000 steps a day. That's nine miles. The women walked about seven miles every day. The average American adult walks about 6,000 steps (three miles) a day.

A man's health can be judged by which he
takes two at a time—pills or stairs.

– Joan Welsh

A LITTLE VERSUS A LOT

The vast majority of people in America are at risk for a myriad of diseases because they don't exercise enough. About two-thirds of all adults in America are not active on a regular basis. As many as a quarter get virtually no exercise at all. It's not just making us fatter as a nation, it's endangering our lives!

If you want to get healthy, exercise is a crucial component. But you don't have to get up before dawn and be the hardest-working guy at the gym to get your body in shape. That's how I did it because that's the way I am. I have to do things full-out. It's in my nature. Not everybody's like that.

Although it may take months of consistent exercise to get fit, every time you exercise, your health improves. "Take a 50-year-old man who is somewhat overweight and typically has moderately elevated blood sugar, triglycerides, or blood pressure," says Stanford's William Haskell. "A single bout of exercise of moderate intensity—like 30 to 40 minutes of brisk walking—will lower those numbers."[29] You will be healthier for every day that you exercise. There are literally hundreds of ways to add more exercise into your life. Every one of them will bring you that much closer to fitness.

---

[29] "Exploding Ten Exercise Myths: If You Can't Exercise Regularly, Why Bother?" Nutrition Action newsletter, www.cspinet.org (August 2004).

NO TIME TO SPARE?

If you don't have time to exercise, try multitasking.

- Can you exercise while you watch TV? If you use oven bags, you can put your dinner in the oven and go for a brisk walk while it is cooking!
- Do you need to spend time with the kids? Work them into your exercise program!
- Don't have time to read motivational or educational material and also exercise? Get books on tape and listen while you walk or work out.

BOOK REFERENCE

In his book, *8 Minutes in the Morning* (Rodale), Jorge Cruise (seen on *Good Morning America* and CNN) shows you how to lose 10, 50, or 100 pounds in just eight minutes a day.

There's always a solution if you really want to find a way. You can do it!

A wealth of research shows that the benefits of exercise are cumulative. That means it's much better to get to the gym three or four days a week, but if you can't work out as much as you'd like, every little bit counts. When something interferes with your exercise plan, there are ways to compensate. You can take the stairs up several flights. If you're fit enough, jog up them! You can park your car at the far end of the parking lot or take a walk around the block as briskly as you can.

Get your heart rate up and sustain it. It will pump blood to your brain, raise your metabolism, and improve your ability to concentrate almost immediately. Dr. Haskell points out that the benefits don't just show up while you're exercising. They continue to improve your health the next day!

The Centers for Disease Control recommends that everyone get at least 30 minutes of moderate activity most days of the week. But any exercise is better than none. Any time you go for a brisk walk or walk up an extra flight of stairs, it's a good thing.

If you're serious about getting fit, of course, you'll need to do better than that. Studies show that people who lose weight and keep it off have one thing in common: exercise. People who have been successful at keeping weight off exercise an average of 3½ hours a week. That's 30 minutes a day, or 40 minutes five days a week.

Some people say that sounds easy, other people say it sounds hard. It all depends on your point of view. Trust me, either way, you have to make it happen.

Nothing tastes as good as being thin feels.

– Anonymous

MAKING IT HAPPEN

Here are a few simple ways to work exercise into your life.

Make it an appointment

When was the last time you found a free hour in the day? A couple months ago? It doesn't happen every week. It certainly doesn't happen every day. Whether you get up 30 minutes earlier to go jogging or use 30 minutes of your lunch break for a brisk walk, put it on your schedule.

Make it fun

Remember how I said it took hard work? It does. But I'll let you in on a little secret: I *love* that about it. Pushing my limits and exceeding my own expectations is something I really enjoy. Circuit training is fun for me. Whatever you choose, it's got to be fun or you'll give it up as soon as possible. The point is to add quality to your life. If you dread working out, it's counterproductive. Find an exercise you really enjoy. Dancing, kick-boxing, fencing, ice skating, jumping rope, hiking, gardening, skiing, racquetball, volleyball, swimming, and even housework are exercises. Pick the ones that are right for you.

Make it social

When you include other people, you increase your chances of success. It's easier to go back to aerobics class on Tuesdays and Thursdays when you've made friends with the people in the class and you know they'll all be there, wondering where you are! It's easier to get yourself to the gym every day when you know your trainer will be waiting for you. Get other people involved.

The human body is made up of some 400 muscles,
evolved through centuries of physical activity.
Unless these are used, they will deteriorate.

– Eugene Lyman Fisk

Pace yourself

One killer workout isn't going to get you fit. It takes steady, consistent effort. When you push too hard, you overtrain. Your muscles get fatigued and your energy plummets. Ease yourself into it at first, until you learn what your body can handle. You may think you should be able to ride an exercise bike for an hour, but it's more realistic to start slowly and work your way up. Ask any trainer. One of the classic mistakes beginners make is to start back in at the same level they used to be at—a month, a year, or even 20 years ago! You'll lose nothing by pacing yourself and you'll gain the ability to sustain your efforts.

WEB REFERENCE
One of the best fitness newsletters around is Tom Venuto's Fitness Renaissance. Venuto calls it the honest, unbiased, information fitness website. And he lives up to that promise. Check it out for yourself at www.fitren.com.

Exercise consistently

Once you get going, don't stop. Every bit of exercise you do is good for you, as I've said. But to really see dramatic changes, you're going to have to stick with a consistent program over the long-term. A smaller consistent effort adds up to a lot more than intense bursts of effort done at random intervals.

WHAT MAKES EXERCISE WORK?

Exercise increases your energy output by using stored calories for extra fuel. Recent studies show that not only does exercise increase metabolism during a workout, but your metabolism is increased for a period of time after exercising, allowing you to burn more calories.

How much exercise is needed to make a difference in your weight depends on the amount and type of activity, and on how much you eat. Aerobic exercise burns body fat. A medium-sized adult needs to walk more than 30 miles to burn up 3,500 calories (the equivalent of one pound of fat). Although that may seem like a lot, you don't have to walk the 30 miles all at once. Walking a mile a day for 30 days will achieve the same result, as long as you don't eat more.

If you consume even 100 calories a day more than your body needs (that's one slice of bread), you will gain approximately 10 pounds in a year.

You can take that weight off—or keep it off—by doing 30 minutes of moderate exercise a day. The combination of exercise and diet offers the most flexible and effective approach to weight control.

If you are going to try cross-country skiing,
start with a small country.

– Anonymous

BOOK REFERENCE

All Star Trainer's Secrets to Maximum Muscle Gain and Maximum Fat Loss in 30 Days **is a comprehensive book filled with valuable information from eleven of the most knowledgeable, sought-after personal trainers. In it, top trainers share their favorite shortcuts to achieving body transformation. But brace yourself—despite the flashy title, this isn't a gimmick-driven book. It's still going to take dedication and hard work to reach your fitness goals. There's no way around that. The more you know, the more direct your path to success. Check it out at www.allstarsecrets.com.**

EXERCISE AND YOUR BRAIN

Every year we hear more chilling stories about brain disease and aging. More than previous generations, we live in dread of losing our mental capacities as we age. But we're in luck. Exercise is proving to be a significant deterrent to reduced brain capacity.

The Beckman Institute at the University of Illinois at Champaign-Urbana recently studied the effects of exercise on the aging brain. They specifically sought out inactive people between the ages of 58 to 78 and started them on a walking program. For three months these people walked three days a week, gradually increasing their time to 45 minutes a day.

A parallel control group of people in the same age group, who were also inactive, participated in toning and stretching exercises, but did nothing aerobic.

The researchers then measured the participants' brain activity with magnetic resonance imaging (MRI). People in the walking group had significantly increased activity in the brain with more intense blood flow to the frontal lobe. That is where our memory and capacity for multitasking resides. The walking group also had a much greater ability to perform tasks that require alertness and attention.[30]

You don't have to be stuck with an out-of-shape body, loss of memory, or inability to think like you used to. Once again, scientists are proving that it's all about choice. You can *choose* to keep your brain healthy and activity into old age. (A lot of the study participants were almost 80!) Exercise will get you in shape and even improve your ability to think clearly. What are you waiting for?

The human body was designed to walk, run, or stop;
it wasn't built for coasting.

– Cullen Hightower

[30] Jackson, Carole, "It's Never Too Late." Bottom Line's Daily Health News (May 18, 2004)

TWELVE OTHER REASONS TO EXERCISE

Losing weight is an American pastime. Except for the minority of people who are thin without working at it, a majority of people in the country are either on a diet, cheating on a diet, or thinking about going on a diet. Increasingly, those same people realize that their only hope of success is to exercise too.

Exercise plays an important role in weight control by increasing energy output. If you do it right, it will use up the extra calories stored in your body as fuel. Not only does exercise increase your metabolism during your workouts, it keeps your metabolism high for hours afterward. So you burn more calories.

Ultimately, the right combination of diet and exercise will make you as strong, lean, and fit as you would ever want to be. It's a matter of knowing what to do, then doing it consistently until you reach your goals. I'm going to be saying a lot more about that throughout this chapter. But if you think you can skip this chapter because you don't have any weight to lose, think again!

The benefits of exercise could fill a book. But here are a dozen from the Nutrition Action Health Newsletter:[31]

Sleep better

Studies have shown than 30 to 40 minutes of brisk walking or moderate aerobics, done four times a week, can measurably improve sleep. As I said earlier, you're likely to notice it the very first night. After a few months of consistent exercise, you'll get so used to sleeping well that, if you miss a few days of exercise and go back to sleeping like you used to, you'll really notice a difference!

Exercise: you don't have time not to.

– Anonymous

[31] "Twelve Other Reasons to Exercise," Nutrition Action Health Newsletter (Jan./Feb. 2000).

- **Reduce gallstones**

Exercise can reduce your likelihood of gallstones by as much as 30 percent. One study showed that women who spent more than 20 hours a week sitting or driving doubled their odds of having gallstone surgery.

- **Lower your risk of colon cancer**

Active people have half the risk of colon cancer that inactive people have.

- **Reduce diverticulitis**

Inactive men have been shown to have 63% greater risk of diverticular disease, which causes inflammation in the colon. Vigorous activities like jogging and running seemed to have the most benefit.

- **Relieve arthritis**

Aerobic or strength-training can reduce pain and joint swelling, if done on a regular basis.

- **Curb anxiety or depression**

Brisk exercise, such as walking or running, releases natural opiates and raises serotonin levels, creating a tangible sense of well-being.

- **Decrease heart disease**

Exercise increases the supply of oxygen to the heart, expands existing arteries, and creates new blood vessels. Physicians believe it may also help prevent blood clots or encourage their breakdown.

- **Lower blood pressure**

If you have high blood pressure, regular aerobic exercise can lower it. If you have normal blood pressure, regular exercise can help keep it normal.

- **Reduce risk of diabetes**

Walking three hours a week has been shown to reduce the risk of diabetes by 40%. The effects are especially powerful if you are overweight or have high blood pressure.

- **Prevent falls and fractures**

Strength exercises can prevent falls and other injuries, especially in the elderly. Balance and core balance exercises reduce injuries by improving strength and reaction time.

- **Reduce prostate problems**

Studies show that men who walked briskly two or three hours a week reduced their odds of an enlarged prostate by 25%.

- **Decrease osteoporosis**

Exercise is good for the bones, as well as muscles. Strength training has been shown to increase bone density, even in middle aged and older people.

HOW MUCH EXERCISE IS ENOUGH? [32]

There's a lot of conflicting exercise advice out there. One week, you hear an expert say that a little moderate exercise, like walking or gardening, is all you need. The next week, a new study comes out "proving" that it takes at least 30 minutes of exercise a day to make any difference. Then, if you stay up late enough, you can see one infomercial after another, promising that you can have killer abs in only 15 minutes, three days a week! Or better yet, you don't have to do anything at all. Just attach a few electrodes to your belly and turn on the machine!

[32] Stenson, Jacqueline. www.msnbc.msn.com (June 2004).

So how much exercise is really enough? Jacqueline Stenson of msnbc.com says it best: "The bottom line is that no one knows the ideal amount of exercise. And one-size-fits-all exercise recommendations may not fit you." The perfect exercise program has to be tailor-made for you. Your age, your health status, your experience, and your fitness goals are all part of the equation.

Do not worry; eat three square meals a day . . . keep your digestion good; exercise; go slow and easy. Maybe there are other things your special case requires to make you happy; but, my friend, these I reckon will give you a good lift.

– Abraham Lincoln

WHAT'S YOUR GOAL?

Before you can choose an exercise program, you have to decide what your goal is. Do you want to lose a spare tire or have more stamina? If you're trying to lose 40 pounds, you'll have to take a more vigorous approach than someone at the ideal weight who wants to stay fit.

According to Jacqueline Stenson, here are some appropriate levels of exercise for some of the more common goals.

Good health

The 1996 Surgeon General's report says that 30 minutes of moderate exercise on most days should be sufficient to ensure good health. If you're reasonably healthy, you may already get this much exercise now. How long do you spend doing ordinary physical activities like vacuuming, washing the car, playing weekend sports, or cleaning up after dinner? This 30 minutes can be broken up into three 10-minute sessions. That makes it very easy to accumulate 30 minutes with small activities every day.

- **Lose weight**

To lose excess weight, that 30 minutes you need for general health isn't going to be enough. The recommendation for losing weight is an hour a day on most days. To get the most benefit from this hour, you will need to do exercise that raises your heart rate and makes you sweat.

- **Look like a bodybuilder**

Housework and gardening are not going to turn you into a bodybuilder. If that were true, the average person would have a killer bod. Weight training is essential for creating a sculpted body. Hard-core fitness enthusiasts and athletes will almost inevitably have to hire a trainer and follow a rigorous program to help monitor their progress and maximize their potential.

The body of man is a machine which winds its own springs.

– J. O. De La Mettrie

BURNING CALORIES

When the amount of calories you eat is equal to the amount of calories you burn, your weight is stable. On the other hand, when you eat more calories than you burn, the extra calories are stored as fat and you gain weight.

One pound of stored fat is equivalent to 3,500 stored calories, which means that if you eat 500 more calories than you need each day *for even a week*, you will gain one pound of body weight.

So, how can you get rid of those unwanted pounds? Most of the people who are able to lose weight and keep it off use a two-pronged approach. This approach involves cutting back on calories slightly and increasing physical exercise.

Let's say your goal is to lose one pound per week. Remember that one pound of stored fat contains 3,500 calories. If you do nothing but cut calories, you will have to eat 500 fewer calories per day to lose one pound a week. For many people, cutting calories this severely is torture, as they feel hungry all of the time and are tempted to cheat.

But, if you increase your physical activity and by doing so burn an extra 250 calories per day, then you need to cut only 250 calories out of your diet to achieve your weight-loss goal of one pound per week!

For the average person, it takes between 25 and 50 minutes to burn 250 calories. A precise determination of how long it takes you to burn up 250 calories depends on your body composition (weight and body fat percentage), but a good estimate can be made by simply counting each minute of non-stressful activity as burning five calories.

Non-stressful activity includes fairly brisk walking and very leisurely swimming. On a treadmill going all-out at 15 METS, a good estimate of caloric expenditure is 15 calories per minute. Although many aerobic machines indicate that approximately 10 calories are burned per minute even at lower levels of activity, this is frequently an overestimate. A good estimate is that between 5 and 10 calories are burned per minute, depending upon your level of activity. This translates to somewhere between 25 and 50 minutes to burn 250 calories.

Exercise has ongoing benefits for weight loss too. When you exercise, you build muscle mass. By increasing your muscle mass (also called lean body mass), you raise your resting metabolic rate, which means that your body burns more calories just to maintain your body temperature and keep vital functions going. And as you build muscle mass you will notice changes in your body shape. Plus, people who exercise often report feeling better and have a more positive outlook.

You can burn 250 calories by walking at a brisk pace for 30 minutes, cycling for about 45 minutes, or running for 20 to 30 minutes. You can also burn extra calories simply by increasing your activity around the house and in your garden. Find a few different activities that you enjoy, and vary your routine from time to time.

I have to exercise in the morning
before my brain figures out what I'm doing.

– Marsha Doble

If possible, pair up with someone of similar endurance level. Exercising with a friend can be more fun and help keep you motivated. If you do not currently exercise, consult a physician before initiating an exercise program.

A vigorous five-mile walk will do more good for an unhappy but otherwise healthy adult than all the medicine and psychology in the world.

– Paul Dudley White

SETTING YOUR GOALS

You would never consider starting a new business without first making a plan. There are too many things to consider. The same is true with exercise. To get the most benefit and make the most gains, you need a plan.

Set clear goals with specific target dates. Getting professional advice is the best way to create appropriate exercise goals. Even if you can't afford a regular trainer, it's possible to consult a trainer to set up your program and check back in with them at regular intervals. Or you can try some of the excellent resources available from online trainers.

Schedule time to exercise. You can get in shape by exercising 3½ hours a week. Working out six days a week, that's just 25 minutes on three days and 45 minutes on the other three days. It's not much time over the course of a week but, believe me, if you don't schedule it, it's never going to happen.

Keep track of your exercise. My trainer provided me with a log to record each session. Be sure to write down what you're doing, so you'll be able to constantly increase your effort and keep making progress.

Movement is a medicine for creating change in a person's physical, emotional, and mental states.

– Carol Welch

NEED A TRAINER?

When you're putting together a workout program, you need a trainer to help get you started. Few things can beat the personal instruction and motivational power of an onsite trainer. But if you can't afford one or want the added benefits this program provides, GlobalFitness (GHF) is a good alternative. It gives you a lot for your money.

GlobalFitness.com has one of the best exercise and fitness programs around. And it's online, waiting for you! This award-winning site will help you get the results you want. A few of the numerous benefits of membership include:

1. 175 video demonstrations of exercises online! You can print them out and take them to the gym with you, so you'll know how to do the exercises when you're there.

2. Protrack 2005, an exercise and nutrition tracking software that helps you keep track of your program.

3. 24-hour access to 30 of the best fitness trainers available. They will answer your questions as you go and help you develop a program tailored to your goals.

Full membership costs $59.95. That is the average cost of one session with a trainer at the gym. A 30-day trial is just $4.95. Go to www.global-fitness.com.

Pain is temporary. Quitting is forever.

– Lance Armstrong

WALK YOUR WAY TO FITNESS

What would we do without researchers to check things out for us? At the University of Tennessee, Knoxville, physiologists studied 80 women between the ages of 40 and 60—exactly the stage in life when people tend to put on extra weight.

They found that the women who averaged 10,000 steps a day had

40% less body fat. Their waists were four to six inches smaller than those of women who walked less than 6,000 steps a day (the national average).

Adding 4,000 steps to your day takes a conscious effort. Most of the women who walked more walked their dogs every day or made a specific effort to walk while doing their errands. As you might guess, the 4,000 additional steps take about 30 minutes a day—exactly what doctors recommend for increased health.

> *A pedestrian is a man in danger of his life.*
> *A walker is a man in possession of his soul.*
>
> – David McCord

A LITTLE EVERY DAY

Here are a few ways you can add in extra steps every day. You'll still have to make a conscious effort to do it—not just a few times a week, but *every single day*—but the effort is comparatively small and the payoff could add years to your life!

- At the mall, spend an extra 15 minutes window shopping.
- At the office, park on the upper level and take the stairs.
- At the movies, park at the far edge of the parking lot and walk to the theater.
- At home, get a dog and walk it every day.
- While you're waiting—for your car to be washed or repaired —take a walk.
- On your break, step outside and walk briskly for 10 minutes.
- As a habit—just before going home from work or just after you get home—take a 15-minute walk. If you associate the walk with a regular activity, you'll be more likely to do it every day.

TWO MORE WAYS TO FIT IN EXERCISE

As you know only too well, time to exercise won't make itself. "I don't have time" is the single most common excuse for not exercising. When you work 40 or more hours a week, have a commute to and from work, and have a busy life outside the office, it's hard to imagine where you'd squeeze in an hour's workout—not to mention preparation and travel time!

According to Michele Stanten of *Prevention* magazine, 77% of Americans say their workouts get ditched when they get busy.[33] Here are two more ways you can fit exercise into your life.

Start small

Your goal may be that optimal 3½ hours a week, but even two hours a week of extra exercise is a solid sign of progress. Next week, add 15 minutes. And soon you'll be up to 3½ hours painlessly.

Do double-duty exercise

You've got to relax and have fun, right? Make two of your exercise hours something playful and enjoyable—riding a bike in the country, belly dancing, taking squash lessons, or walking briskly while you shop.

EXERCISE: WHAT'S YOUR EXCUSE?

Once someone succeeds in getting fit, other people tend to assume it came naturally to them. In my case, nothing is further from the truth. Before I started my exercise regimen, I had plenty of excuses:

1. Lack of time
2. Lack of energy
3. Lack of money
4. Lack of interest
5. Lack of past success
6. Lack of knowledge
7. Lack of need

Use it or lose it.

– American proverb

[33] Stanten, Michele, *Prevention* (May 2004)

There is no end of possible excuses, if you really want some. Most of us are stopped or waylaid by excuses that never fully form in our heads. We put it off, we tell ourselves we'll do it later, but we're really just skirting the issue. If we really stopped to think about our excuses, they'd fall apart.

Look at number 1 on my list: lack of time. I was working a grueling schedule, there's no doubt about that. But when I really wanted it, I found a way to work out: getting up early and scheduling it like a business appointment. That's the way it is with excuses.

What's your excuse? You've seen the top seven excuses on my list. Take a moment right now to think about it, then write down the top seven on yours.

Now, write down a solution for each one of them. The really remarkable thing is how quickly a solution will come to mind! It makes you realize that nine times out of ten an excuse is just an excuse.

TOP EIGHT REASONS FOR NOT WORKING OUT

Prevention magazine reports that, in an Australian study, women said that these are the top reasons that the best laid plans for working out were interrupted:

1. Having a baby
2. Getting married
3. Demands of single parenthood
4. Getting a new job
5. Getting a divorce
6. Working too much
7. Pressures at work
8. Going back to school

All of these are legitimate interruptions to a busy life. There's no question about that. Now, can you think of workout *solutions* for each of these situations?

It is remarkable how one's wits
are sharpened by physical exercise.

– Pliny the Younger

YOUR CHALLENGE

Once I made the choice to take charge of my own fitness and create the body I wanted, amazing changes took place in my life. A year later I had the body I'd hoped for and, even better, I understood how to keep it! Even more importantly, the hard work and determination that had made my success possible had changed me for the better. The success had strengthened my character, improved my focus, and boosted my self-esteem. I felt more alive and empowered than I had in years.

What would happen if you did the same thing? What if you started right now?

I challenge you to take charge of your fitness. Set up a program that will make you look and feel 10 years younger, that will *completely* transform your body, once and for all. Make it your goal that one year from today, you will have achieved these goals.

I'll let you in on a little secret: The result is going to be *much* better than you think. Not only will you feel better and have a new level of health and vitality, you'll also serve as an inspiration for everyone around you!

Success is contagious. People will look at you and say, "If you can do it, so can I!" You'll open the door to new possibilities for everyone around you. The personal growth and happiness that spread out from my own efforts astounded me. I was just trying to lose that embarrassing spare tire and get in shape. On the way, I inadvertently improved the lives of my friends and family, by inspiring them to try harder and do more with their own lives too!

Getting in shape was great. But helping others make their lives better was priceless.

A wonderful experience awaits you. Don't sell yourself short. You can do this. And when you do, the outcome is going to be amazing. Don't put it off another minute. Start today!

Physical fitness is not only one of the most important keys to a healthy body, it is the basis of dynamic and creative intellectual activity.

– John F. Kennedy

CHAPTER 9

Choosing to Live Longer

May you live all the days of your life!

– Irish proverb

In this generation, our life expectancy is expected to leap forward by another 10 to 40 years. New research in healthier eating habits, micronutrients, advanced supplements, exercise regimens, genome research, and other enormous breakthroughs in medical science hold the promise that we will be able to live much longer and more vibrant lives.

Already, more of us are living past 100 years old. In 1940, there were just 3,700 centenarians (people over 100) in the United States. By 1990, there were 61,000. The National Institute of Health predicts that in just a few years, by 2020, there will be 214,000 people over 100 in America alone.

My friend and colleague, David Solie, has identified nine things that increase your odds for living that long. He calls the 100-year mark "the gold standard of longevity."[34] If you could live in vibrant health, who wouldn't want to live to be at least 100? To read Solie's booklet on this subject online, go to www.Secondopin.com and click Centenarian Markers.

---

[34] Solie, David. "Longevity and Underwriting: The Centenarian Markers," www.RiskTutor.com (September 2003).

QUIZ: WILL YOU LIVE TO BE 100?

Today, most people will live to be 85 years of age or more. Those who actively improve their health and get exercise can add decades of quality years to their lives. Those who put it off—never go on the diet, never quit smoking, never get daily exercise—can literally subtract years from their lives.

Take a free quiz to evaluate what your odds are of living to be 100. The Living to be 100 Healthspan Calculator (at www.livingto100.com) will let you know where you stand. If things don't look good, there's still time to improve. If you get a great score on the quiz, keep improving anyway. Who knows? You might make it to 120!

The tragedy of life is not that it ends so soon,
but that we wait so long to begin it.

– W. M. Lewis

INDICATORS OF LONG LIFE

There's no reason to live a long time if you're going to be feeble and miserable. So when I refer to longevity in this book, you can assume I'm talking about what David Solie calls "enhanced longevity." The centenarians he studied did not suffer from long periods of disability or chronic illness. They led healthy lives with a brief illness before their deaths.

What did these people have in common?

Good use of health care

Medical science has made many advances, but if you don't make use of them you won't have the benefit of those breakthroughs! Check-ups, vaccines, screening tests, and preventative medicine are the first things on the list if you want to live a long and healthy life.

Life well spent is long.

– Leonardo da Vinci

A safe level of cholesterol

Dr. Kenneth H. Cooper, author of *Controlling Cholesterol the Natural Way* (Bantam), says it's possible for many people to lower their cholesterol without taking prescription drugs. The right diet and supplements are often enough to lower cholesterol to safer levels. (Be sure to consult with your doctor to see which of these alternatives might be effective for you.)

Low-fat diet: Limiting total fat calories to 30% or less is vital. Make sure that saturated fats make up no more than 10% of your total calories.

Fiber: Eating seven to eight grams of soluble fiber every day can lower your cholesterol by 5 to 8%.

Psyllium: Added to food as a powder or taken in capsules, psyllium is a great source of fiber. Studies show that 3 grams of psyllium a day can lower cholesterol by 15%.

Bran: Eating three ounces of oat or rice bran a day may improve your ratio of "bad" (LDL) to "good" (HDL) cholesterol by as much as 24%.

Fish: Eating oily fish such as salmon, tuna, or mackerel once a week can reduce your risk for heart attack by 52%.

Dr. Cooper also recommends three supplements that have been shown to directly affect cholesterol levels:

Vitamin E: At least 400 IU of the natural form (d-alpha-tocopherol) a day.

Vitamin C: At least 500 mg, twice a day.

Niacin: This is a B vitamin. At least 1.5 to 3 grams a day can lower LDL by 15 to 30%, as well as raising HDL by 10 to 40%.

A MARGARINE THAT LOWERS CHOLESTEROL!

Benecol is a new spread that lowers cholesterol as effectively as some drugs. Eating three tablespoons of benecol a day can lower LDL by 14% If you'd rather take a pill, benecol is also available in gel tablets.

For more information on this important subject, get Dr. Cooper's book, *Controlling Cholesterol the Natural Way,* or go to www.bottomlinesecrets.com.

When you think about it,
what other choice is there but to hope?
We have two options:
give up, or fight like hell.

– Lance Armstrong

Longevity genes

You knew this was coming, didn't you? There are definitely advantages to having people in your family tree who lived long lives. Some genetic lines help people slow the aging process and reduce their vulnerability to disease. For now, you either have it or you don't. But scientists are actively trying to identify the genes. Keep living well and you may be around long enough to benefit when they find these genes and learn to extend all our lives.

Strong immune system

People with longevity genes tend to have naturally strong immune systems. But nutrition can strengthen or weaken anyone's immune system. Good nutrition can directly enhance your longevity. A number of vitamins and minerals play a vital role in building up your immune system:

Zinc	Folic acid
Selenium	Vitamin A
Iron	Vitamin B
Copper	Vitamin D

SUPPLEMENTS TO WATCH OUT FOR

Vitamins and supplements have proven to be a wonderful asset to improving our health. As BottomlineDaily.com points out, not all supplements are safe or effective. It's important to be well informed about what you're taking. Sometimes, checking with your doctor or a naturopath is the best course of action. You can find an experienced naturopath in your area by going to www.naturopathic.org.

In the meantime, here are some supplements that the doctors at *Consumer Reports* and Bottomline Daily recommend watching out for:

1. **Androstenedione** (aka "andro"). It corrects estrogen or testosterone levels, but can have serious side effects, such as increased risk of cancer and reduced HDL (good) cholesterol.

2. **Aristolochic acid.** This is the *only* supplement that *Consumer Reports* says is "definitely hazardous." Don't take it. It's carcinogenic and can cause organ failure.

3. **Chaparral** is a natural antibiotic and antioxidant. It is difficult to use properly. Take it only under the advice of a doctor or naturopath.

4. **Germander** is listed as a common remedy for gout or fever. It is difficult to use properly. Take it only under the advice of a doctor or naturopath.

5. **Pennyroyal** is popular as a natural stimulant. It is difficult to use properly. Take it only under the advice of a doctor or naturopath.

6. **Glandular extracts.** *Consumer Reports* advises against the use of organ or glandular extracts because of the risk of mad cow disease.

7. **Scullcap**. This is often used as a sedative, but it can cause liver damage.

8. **Yohimbe.** It is a natural aphrodisiac, used like Viagra. It has the same potential side effects as Viagra: changes in blood pressure, heartbeat irregularities, and even heart attack.
9. **Bitter orange.** This is a natural stimulant. *Consumer Reports* advises caution, since it can cause high blood pressure and heart arrhythmia.
10. **Kava.** Often used as a drink, it is a calming, anti-anxiety agent. Unfortunately, most commercial preparations alter its chemical properties. Now it can cause abnormal liver function.

Keep in mind that many of the most potent drugs in the world are derived from botanicals, which can be called "natural." Even the chemicals in our own bodies can kill us if we have too much of them. "Natural" doesn't mean safe. Take care about what you put in your body.

DR. WHITAKER'S VITAMINS AND MINERALS

For more than 25 years, Dr. Julian Whitaker has been helping people to live longer, healthier lives by combining the most powerful conventional medicine recommendations with the best alternative medicine approaches. His website is a rich resource for health information. You can subscribe to his newsletter for the latest health information. For years, I have been taking his vitamin and mineral program with great success. I highly recommend it. You can find it on his website at www.drwhitaker.com.

Finish each day and be done with it. You have done what you could; some blunders and absurdities have crept in; forget them as soon as you can. Tomorrow is a new day; you shall begin it serenely and with too high a spirit to be encumbered with your old nonsense.

– Ralph Waldo Emerson

BOOK REFERENCE

Too many remedies and cures to choose from? Bottom Line's *Complete Book of Integrated Health Solutions* shows you how to integrate these 21 different approaches to health:

- Conventional medicine
- Vitamin and mineral supplements
- Chinese herbal medicine
- Homeopathy
- Ayurvedic (Indian) medicine
- Biofeedback
- Qi gong
- Bodywork
- Tai chi
- Aromatherapy
- Nutritional therapies
- Naturopathy
- Acupuncture
- Western herbal medicine
- Chiropractic
- Meditation and prayer
- Yoga
- Massage
- Hypnotherapy
- Visualization
- Music therapy

For a free 30-day preview, go to www.bottomlinesecrets.com. I recommend subscribing to their free newsletter while you're at it. I've been enjoying it and benefiting from its advice for years.

Regular exercise

Centenarians always live active lives. Consistent physical activity and exercise are well-established ways to add years to your life. When you start a regular exercise program, plan to keep it up well into old age. It will improve your blood circulation, fend off disease, and help you sleep better.

The question is not whether we will die, but how we will live.

– Joan Borysenko

TIPS FOR INSOMNIA

If you can't get to sleep, Bottom Line health expert Jamison Starbuck, ND, says that prescription drugs will only knock you out. Natural treatments can get to the cause of your insomnia.

Stress, pain, and hormonal irregularity are often the culprits. Relaxation at bedtime by listening to soothing music or taking a warm epsom salt bath can do wonders. Here are a few other alternatives:

Magnesium. A magnesium citrate supplement (300 mg), along with a homeopathic version of magnesium called Mag Phos 6X can help you relax.

Calms Forté (Hyland's). This formula combines passion flower, oats, and chamomile. It reduces anxiety and calms your mind.

Valerian. This herb helps with stress-related insomnia. Try it in a liquid form at bedtime.

Melatonin. A small dose of melatonin (0.5 mg) can be sufficient at first. Then increase it slightly after five days. (Dr. Starbuck advises caution, since long-term studies on melatonin have yet to be done. It's always best to discuss it with a medical professional.)

Normal weight

Those who live the longest, healthiest lives do it at a normal weight. Not only are they likely to be more fit, but they are less prone to suffer from diabetes, heart disease, or other illnesses.

With decrepitude, longevity has overshot the mark.

– Mason Cooley

Not smoking

The single thing that most centenarians the world over have in common is that they are non-smokers. Not only does non-smoking increase your life expectancy, it also reduces the years you might live with disability or illness. Beware of secondhand smoke as well. It can be just as noxious as smoking yourself.

HELP FOR SMOKERS

Did you know that acupuncture can help you quit smoking? The minute you quit smoking, you reduce your risk of early death from lung cancer, heart attack, or stroke. You also increase your health on a day-to-day basis, not to mention your ability to walk up a flight of stairs! To find a licensed acupuncturist in your area, call the American Academy of Medical Acupuncture at 800-521-2262 or visit www.medicalacupuncture.org.

Social connections

People live longer, more healthy lives when they are connected to family, friends, and social groups. Living in isolation can lead to depression and a shorter life.

Enjoy life. There's plenty of time to be dead.

– Anonymous

Good attitude

Researchers almost always remark that centenarians seem to be happier than other people. They are simply good at managing their lives. Optimism, humor, and calm are their personality traits. As David Solie says, "Their mental fitness parallels their physical fitness, and they are consistent in their dedication to both."[35]

Die young at the oldest age possible.

– Anonymous

---

35 Solie, David. "Longevity and Underwriting: The Centenarian Markers," www.RiskTutor.com (September 2003).

Personal responsibility

Centenarians have a sense of a greater responsibility to the world beyond themselves. Many have a spiritual faith. All of them share the ability to accept responsibility for their lives in the bigger context of the world around them.

> **TAKE A POWER NAP**
>
> A new CD by Speed Sleep® will help you fall into a deep sleep in minutes. You can wake up refreshed after a perfectly timed 25-minute nap and boost your energy and mental alertness. Now that I've tried it, I highly recommend it to you. Check it out at speedsleep.com.

PREVENTATIVE MEASURES

Many of the advances in modern medicine allow doctors to nip things in the bud. Early detection of cancer, for instance, enormously improves your odds of survival. Other diseases and illnesses can be treated much more effectively if they're discovered early.

Unfortunately, many of the symptoms aren't noticeable until the problem has been around for awhile. Improvements in screening technologies give us a new advantage in this area. CT scans, PET scans, and full-body scans are becoming more and more popular because of their ability to detect problems even before they produce symptoms.

CT scans

According to the American Cancer Society, CT (computed tomography) scans take X-rays of your body from many angles, then piece together a whole portrait of the inside of your body. They can quickly reveal abnormal growths.

PET scans

With a PET (positron emission tomography) scan, glucose (sugar) containing very low levels of radiation is injected into your body. Since glucose tends to accumulate more in cancer cells than in ordinary cells, the PET scan is better at finding very small deposits of cancer cells.

Full-body scans

The full-body scan detects early signs of cancer, heart disease, aortic aneurysms, gallbladder stones, kidney stones, osteoporosis, arthritis, and as many as 100 diseases, years in advance. While some doctors feel that a full-body scan is a needless expense for someone without symptoms, Dr. Harvey Eisenberg, who offers the scans at the HealthView Centre for Preventative Medicine in Newport Beach, California, says that most people who have the scan feel that they are more in control of their body. They tend to be people who would "rather know" and start doing something about it, if an early sign of disease is detected.

In addition to these types of screenings, there are numerous blood screens and other procedures available now that were unfamiliar even a few years ago. Great advances are being made in this area. Ask your doctor which ones may be right for you.

EARLY DETECTION OF CANCER

A new blood test called anti-malignan antibody (AMAS) is being used to identify an antibody that is created by your own immune system in response to the presence of cancer cells. It allows for early detection. With some cancers, like prostate cancer, early detection gives you a 99% likelihood of a cure. Ask your doctor about the AMAS test. For more information, see www.agora-inc.com.

Believe that life is worth living and your belief will help create the fact.

– William James

Life consists not of holding good cards but of playing those you hold well.

– Josh Billings

CHOOSING OPTIMAL HEALTH

Whole libraries of books have been written about how to get healthy. In the space available in this book, I've shared with you some of the things that have helped make me more healthy and improved my life in measurable ways.

Not only have I gotten into the best shape of my life by using this information, but I have also dramatically reduced my cholesterol and lowered my blood pressure without the use of prescription drugs. All of these things have increased the likelihood of my living a long and vibrantly healthy life. Read this information carefully. It really works. Go to the websites, go get the books, and find out as much as you can. Take action on what you've learned. And you too can improve your chances for a long, healthy life.

As Mahatma Gandhi once said, "Live as if you were to die tomorrow. Learn as if you were to live forever."

QUICK STRESS REDUCTION

My former yoga instructor taught me a quick and quiet way to reduce stress on the spot. You can do it any time and any place. Just pause for a moment and take three deep cleansing breaths. I've started taking three deep breaths every time I get into a stressful situation and it really helps.

Fear less, hope more;
Whine less, breathe more;
Talk less, say more;
Hate less, love more;
And all good things are yours.

– Swedish proverb

Part 4

BE WEALTHY

The real measure of your wealth is how much you'd be worth if you lost all your money.

– Anonymous

CHAPTER 10

Choosing True Wealth

True wealth is family, friends, and loving what you do.

– Debbi Fields, founder of
Mrs. Fields' Cookies

I agree with Debbi Fields that family, friends, and loving what you do are important aspects of true wealth, but I would add health to her definition. Good health is one of our most precious assets. Without it, our lives are shorter and we have less vitality with which to enjoy ourselves every day.

In the preceding chapters we've discussed all of the above, because these are the elements of *true* wealth. It is the sum of happiness, health, and financial well-being.

Do you want to know what wealth is?

Happiness + Health = Wealth

It's cumulative. As you build on each element, the outcome will be more than the sum of the parts.

- Surround yourself with people you love. Give them everything you've got. Let them know every day how much you appreciate and treasure them.

- Then guard your health. Stay abreast of the new discoveries about good health and longevity. Don't just read about them—put them to work in your life! If you're overweight, lose weight. If you're not exercising and eating right, start doing so now!

- And learn as much as you can about creating financial security. Start with a job you love as your foundation. Then make use of the advice in this book to diversify your interests and build a stable future for yourself and future generations.

If you do each of these things, your life will be brimming with joy, vitality, and true wealth. No one is keeping you from living a more vibrant life. The choices you make every year, every week, every hour are making the life you lead.

If something's wrong, if something's missing, there's no one else to blame. It's up to you to create true wealth in your life.

BOOK REFERENCE

Brian Tracy is one of the world's most renowned wealth builders. His book, *21 Success Secrets of Self-Made Millionaires*, shows you how to become a millionaire in one generation—starting from nothing. According to *USA Today*, the book "succinctly sums up why some people are going places and others are not."

Among other things, this book will show you how to:

- Increase your income
- Achieve your goals
- Eliminate your debts
- Realize your full potential
- Achieve complete financial security

It's a great wealth-building book, from an expert who consistently offers solid advice and inspiration.

YOU CAN GET THERE FROM HERE!

Some of you reading this book are hedging your bets even now. You've experienced moments of happiness—we all have. Sometimes life just sneaks up on you and makes you laugh or fills your heart with joy. All of us have inexplicably felt like singing or have fallen wholeheartedly in love. So happiness, even when it's fleeting, is familiar.

Most of us know what it's like to be healthy, too—even if we have to think back to the time when we were kids. When we're young, we can make all kinds of wrong choices and our bodies bounce back. Kids are so full of energy, they can hardly keep themselves from running from one activity to the next! Most of us have experienced that full bloom of health.

But wealth? That's another story. How often have you felt truly wealthy?

If we put it purely in financial terms for a moment, how often have you felt financially secure? When was the last time you worried about money? Do you go to bed at night, knowing you could lose your job tomorrow and still be safe, financially?

Are you like countless Americans, who live from paycheck to paycheck, afraid to think about the future because the financial road you're on is leading nowhere? Maybe you've begun to make some financial preparations, but you don't really know how much money you'll need to send the kids to college or how soon you'll be able to retire. Do you feel that you might be on track, but without clear information, it's hard to feel secure?

There are solutions to all of these situations. If you prioritize the issue of financial security and set some clear-cut goals, you can create a plan that will lead to financial success. Thanks to the Internet, the most knowledgeable experts in the world are available to you at the click of a mouse. Even if you have never known financial security in your life, you can get there from here.

> *You aren't wealthy until you have something money can't buy.*
>
> – Garth Brooks

I have been a chartered financial consultant for 20 years. During that time, I've continually educated myself about the wide variety of financial options available. I have personally invested in every form of stock, bonds, annuities, commodities, REITs, real estate, and everything else you can think of. Some proved to be profitable, others did not, so I can attest that there are countless ways to achieve your goals.

These years have helped me appreciate the complexity and uniqueness of every individual's financial needs. I would be derelict in my duties if I were to make recommendations in this chapter on a wholesale basis. Without knowing your individual situation, it doesn't make sense for me to give you financial advice. Rather, I will do what I have done in previous chapters. I will give you the tools and resources to educate yourself, so you can explore your many options for financial achievement.

Few of us get a financial education in school or anywhere else. We normally spend more time planning a vacation every year than we do on our financial future. I will point you in the right direction in this chapter. I'll let you in on some of the best, most comprehensive and reliable resources I've found in my 20 years as a financial consultant, so you can make good use of them, as I have. Then it's up to you to find out what you need to know, and act accordingly.

WHAT ARE YOU WORTH?
CNNMoney.com provides a net worth calculator that will quickly determine your net worth. It's a good idea to regularly calculate your net worth to track your financial progress. Go to cgi.money.cnn.com/tools/networth/networth.html.

You must take control of your financial future. Creating what you want financially is no less important than creating happiness and health in your life. And it's just as possible.

You can have financial wealth. You can have happiness and health as well. And when you bring all of these elements into your life, you'll know the true wealth I'm talking about.

WEB REFERENCE

Robert G. Allen, author of some of the most successful financial books in history, and Mark Victor Hansen, coauthor of the *Chicken Soup for the Soul* series, teamed up to write the excellent bestselling book, *The One Minute Millionaire.*

It teaches a simple system to control your finances. You will learn how to invest your money, create multiple streams of lifetime income, and leave a financially secure future for your loved ones.

Now, you can have the benefits of years of experience and insight in a free, bimonthly e-zine, full of tips for increasing your wealth. Learn more at www.oneminutemillionaire.com.

What you don't know about how money works
is costing you a fortune.

– Steven L. Down

HOW RICH DO YOU HAVE TO BE?

One of the most respective financial experts today is Jean Chatzky of *Money* magazine and the *Today* show. Her website, JeanChatzky.com, is an excellent resource for the latest financial information. In her most recent book, *You Don't Have to Be Rich*, Chatzky reinforces the important idea that I want you to be sure to understand: "Money doesn't have to be a source of stress—it can be the path to comfort and financial freedom it was always meant to be."[36]

It's possible to manage your money in a way that will make you feel good about your life. Whether you're starting out with a rudimentary knowledge of money management or a fairly sophisticated under-

[36] JeanChatzky.com (August 2004).

standing of finance, you can learn to make smart, confident, effective choices that give you the financial power you need.

Chatzky's research shows that, when it comes to happiness, money does make a difference. (You always knew that, right?) But it doesn't make *as much* of a difference as you might think. And the real surprise is that money can cause a lot more unhappiness than many other things in your life. As Chatzky puts it: "Even when it's working in your favor, money can't make you completely happy. But it can—without a doubt—make you miserable." [37]

Of all the things that can make us unhappy, Chatzky found that money was the worst. When something as important to our survival as money is endangered, it creates an awful feeling that our lives are out of our control. Few things can throw us into a state of unhappiness in the same way. But, according to the research, the *amount* of money we have is less important than the feeling that we are in control of our money.

In other words, you don't have to be rich. When asked about the rewards of accumulating "things," I often think of the great lyrics from *Evita,* "They are illusions, not the solutions they promise to be."

Managing your money well is the key to developing an increasing sense of confidence and control when it comes to money. By educating yourself, getting good advice, and following a sound plan, you can readily achieve these goals. People do it every day. But I'll be honest with you, there are thousands more who don't.

He that waits upon fortune is never sure of a dinner.

– Benjamin Franklin

Without a rich heart, wealth is an ugly beggar.

– Ralph Waldo Emerson

[37] JeanChatzky.com (August 2004).

WHAT IF YOU DO NOTHING?

The alternative to taking charge of your financial future is pretty grim. Consider these statistics. In this year alone, more people will go bankrupt than will suffer a heart attack, be diagnosed with cancer, or graduate from college. At a time when the divorce rate is rising to unprecedented heights, more Americans will file for bankruptcy than will file for divorce.[38]

Over 50% of Americans say they really don't have enough money to handle a financial crisis. As many as 56% can't pay their credit cards off every month. More than 40% save less than 5% of their annual income and have no idea how much money they need to save to reach their financial goals.[39] According to the American Bar Association, 70% of all Americans die without a will.

Considering these figures, it's not surprising that 33% don't even want to think about retirement because it's too depressing. And 60% say they're worried about their financial situation.[40]

These figures are discouraging. But keep in mind, except in unusual circumstances, these problems are avoidable. Most of them are based on lack of knowledge about the possibilities. I've said it before, but I'll say it again here: Knowledge is power.

If you want power over your money, you can have it. Read on.

WILL YOU BE AMONG THE HAVES OR HAVE NOTS?

According to the U.S. Census Bureau, the wealthiest people in the country in 1973 had a 44% share of the total income in the U.S. But times are changing. In the 30 years since, the rich are getting richer and the poorer are getting poorer. The top 20% of the people in the country today are making a 50% share of the total income in the U.S. The middle ground is rapidly disappearing. Choosing wealth has never been more important than it is today.

[38] Herbert, Bob. "Admit We Have a Problem," *The New York Times* op-ed (August 9, 2004).
[39, 40] www.jeanchatzky.com (August 2004).

MASLOW'S HIERARCHY OF (FINANCIAL) NEEDS

Although Maslow didn't create the list below, his famous Hierarchy of Human Needs can be directly applied to your own financial needs. This list gives you an idea of the stages of growth you can expect on your way to wealth. It's tough to move to the higher financial level if you can't put food on the table. The best solution is to start at the bottom and work your way up, making sure that you build the strong base you need to establish so you can safely move to the next level.

Self-actualization

- Achievement of your personal potential
- Ability to take higher risks to increase net worth
- Confidence in money management

Self-esteem

- Increased financial acumen
- Consistent capital growth
- The knowledge and skill to get an above-average return on investments

Affiliation

- Ability to protect the safety of your principal
- Growth of financial relationships
- Financial provision for multi-generations

Security

- Financial safety and stability
- Income secured against disability or death
- Retirement provided for

Physiological

- Provision for food, shelter, clothing
- Insurance protections for property
- Basic, survival-level income

All of these needs are important and you are fully capable of meeting each one of them. Begin by learning as much as possible, getting the advice you need, and putting your strategy in place. Then, by taking consistent action to reach your goals, you can steadily make your way up the hierarchy and meet your greatest needs. No one is born with financial savvy. It has to be learned. Make everything you learn a building block to your success.

Success is not to be measured by
how much material wealth is possessed,
but whether you are able to create
at will what you need.

– Paramhansa Yogananda

Today the greatest single source of wealth
is between your ears.

– Brian Tracy

CHAPTER 11

Choosing Your Road to Wealth

Success is never final.

– Winston Churchill

There are many roads to financial wealth. For every person who has made a fortune on Internet stocks, there are many more who have lost money. For everyone who has acquired wealth through luck—by inheriting a fortune, winning a the lottery, or investing in a short-lived trend—there are millions more who have made it by taking small, persistent, well-informed steps toward their goals.

Why not put the odds in your favor by taking those initial steps now? If your rich aunt leaves you a fortune or you win the Lotto later, so much the better. By that time, you'll know what to do with the money.

In the meantime, here are a few basic principles to get you started. As you learn more, you'll be able build on these principles in new and exciting ways.

TIME-TESTED PRINCIPLES

1. Spend less.

You may be surprised to learn that you can often do this without reducing your standard of living. Little things add up more quickly than you'd think. Ask yourself, for instance, how much you spend on frivolous magazines every month. Not the ones you really enjoy or learn from, but the ones you thumb through quickly and discard. If you stopped buying them, or any of the myriad of small things that you don't really need, would it truly impact your quality of life? Keep a journal of what you spend, then go through it and see what you could live without. Placing those funds in a long-term investment could result in significant amount in the long run.

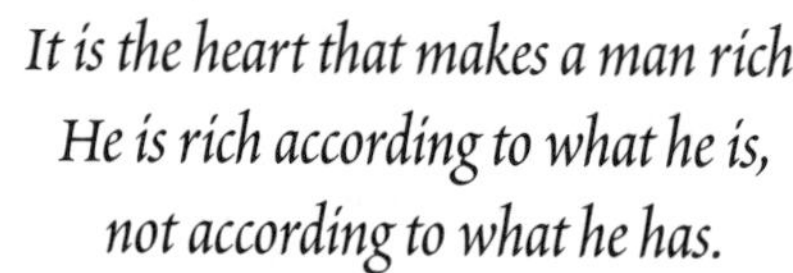

It is the heart that makes a man rich.
He is rich according to what he is,
not according to what he has.

– Henry Ward Beecher

BEFORE YOU SPEND MONEY!

The next time you are tempted to spend money on something that's not in your budget—or would require dipping into funds you've earmarked for something else—ask yourself:

- Is this more important than my financial goals?
- Can I do without it?
- Do I need this or want it?
- Am I buying this for emotional reasons? And, if so, can I do something else to meet that emotional need instead?
- Do I already have one of these?
- Can I get it more cheaply elsewhere?
- Can I rent, borrow, or buy one used?
- Will I still want it 15 minutes from now?

- (Refrain) Is it more important than my financial goals?

2. Reduce your debt.

Heavy credit card debt can make your finances more precarious. With high interest rates, you pay many times more for every dollar you owe. Reducing this debt is a top priority. Many financial experts recommend making extra payments on your credit cards before putting money in your savings account. Whether you choose that route or not, carrying a balance on your cards is an insidious expense—one to watch out for! For help with this, visit www.myvesta.com.

3. Make a plan.

Just as you need a plan for dieting and exercise, you need a plan to create wealth. If you don't have a plan, with action steps that lead to your goal, you leave your success up to chance. Decide what you need. Figure out how to get it. Then take the steps to reach your goal. Because the options for creating financial wealth are so varied, it makes sense to get good advice from a reliable financial advisor who can help you create a realistic plan that will drive your financial success.

Those who understand interest, earn it.
Those who don't, pay it.

– Old saying

4. Put your money to work.

The greatest financial success is in making your money do all the work, without you having to generate income from a job. Once you are creating enough passive income for you and your family to live comfortably for generations, you will have reached an admirable peak of success. Why not be among the wealthy people who keep working just because they love what they do? Financial advisors can show you how to reach this goal. Don't leave it up to chance!

At moneycentral.msn.com, Terry Savage points out that many people don't recognize the power of compound interest.

If you are earning earned income, you can open a Roth IRA with a maximum $3,000-a-year contribution (about $58 a week). Make this

> **BOOK REFERENCE**
> **Two of the best books around for investors starting out are Eric Tyson's books, *Investing for Dummies* and *Personal Finance for Dummies* (Dimensions). They are well organized, easy to skim, and filled with solid information that will lay the groundwork for the financial education you will soon be building.**

same investment for 30 years and, if historical stock market averages hold, you will have more than $500,000.

In 50 years, the same annual investment would equal $5.2 million, according to the MSN Money's Savings Calculator. Do you know anyone in their twenties or thirties who should hear about this right away? With life expectancy increasing at unprecedented rates, who knows? Even a person in their fifties might conceivably end up living another 40 or 50 years. Wouldn't you be glad to have $5.2 million at any age—especially when it only cost you $58 a week?

5. Create diversity.

As any reputable advisor will tell you, your greatest financial security will come from diversity. With good advice, you can create the right balance of many basic elements: home ownership, savings, stocks, bonds, cash investments, and retirement accounts. Add to that your other specific goals: sending your kids to college, taking a sabbatical, traveling abroad. Whatever your dreams entail, you are likely to be much better off with a variety of investments.

6. Maintain a safety net.

We can never plan for something unexpected. We can only be sure that unforeseen hardships will occur. Financial experts say that saving a minimum of three months' income makes a healthy safety net. Six months, naturally, is better, and a full year is the most sensible safety net. Before you have created enough money to live on without working or provided your family with multiple generations of wealth, you would be well advised to work on providing yourself with a solid safety net for the future.

7. Guard your nest egg.

Using your 401(k), IRA, or other savings to pay for a new car or a vacation or any other short-term expense will deplete your nest egg more quickly than you imagine. Don't give into this temptation. It's the perfect example of that old saying, "One step forward, two steps back." We think of someone doing that dance as being stuck. They're actually moving *backwards!* Start cutting into your nest egg for miscellaneous things and you'll be going nowhere fast.

8. Strive for independence.

As much as possible, rely on yourself, not the government, to provide for your retirement. There is no guarantee that Social Security benefits will be remotely able to meet your needs. Furthermore, don't rely on the job you have now either. Studies show that the average American will change careers many times during the course of their adult life. It only makes sense to strive for the kind of financial security that will be independent of those potential changes.

9. Continue to educate yourself.

Keep learning as much as you can about finances. Learn about your options for investing. To become more knowledgeable about investments, check out Vanguard's PlainTalk® brochures, which provide more basic introductory information to lay the groundwork for continued exploration.[41] You can learn more about these financial strategies at the award-winning website, www.vanguard.com.

WEB REFERENCE

The National Association of Investors Corporation is a nonprofit, volunteer organization dedicated to investment education. You can find out more at www.better-investing.com.

Over the years, I have found Vanguard to be a rich source of investment information. These professionals will give you a host of

41 Adapted from "Ten Time-tested Rules for Financial Success," www.vanguard.com (August 2004).

tools to help you take charge of your money. The articles are written by well-informed financial experts, and their investment counselors have a solid reputation for helping individuals, as well as institutions, at all levels. I share them with you now because they've been a great asset to me.

It is not the man who has too little,
but the man who craves more, that is poor.

– Seneca

WHERE DOES THE MONEY GO?

In their bestselling book, *The Millionaire Next Door*, Thomas Stanley and William Danko made people reconsider what they thought they knew about wealth. They interviewed a cross-section of 1,115 millionaires from all around the country. A majority of these millionaires were living quiet, low-key lives. They didn't spend their money on luxury cars or mansions. In fact, they rightly suspected that some of the flashier millionaires, cruising around urban areas in limos, were actually living beyond their means!

The group Stanley and Danko interviewed had become wealthy without much flash at all. Their financial wealth was the result of hard

BOOK REFERENCE

Andrew Tobias's book, *Only Investment Guide You'll Ever Need* (Harcourt-Brace, 2001), is a bestselling classic that has sold over a million copies. Fully updated, it is a must-have for anyone who wants to manage their money more effectively. As financial advisors have known for years, this book does not provide a scheme for getting rich quickly. Its wisdom lies in its common-sense strategies for long-term success. Tobias covers everything from paying off your credit cards, researching items online before you buy them, and saving money, to more subjective advice, like being careful who you trust when it comes to money. It's good advice.

work, planning, perseverance, and self-discipline. In many cases, they were "compulsive savers and investors."

Stanley and Danko identified seven traits they had in common:

1. They spent much less than they earned.
2. They learned to efficiently allocate their time, energy, and money toward building wealth.
3. They put a higher priority on financial independence than social status.
4. They didn't turn to their parents for financial help.
5. Their own adult children were financially self-sufficient.
6. They learned to act on sound financial opportunities.
7. They selected the right occupations for themselves.

If there's one thing that shouts out from this list it's that these people are *living consciously*. They haven't left their happiness, health, or wealth up to chance. They see it as their own responsibility. They've taken charge. Every time you save money, rather than spending it, you put yourself in control.

When your money does the work for you, you can go for years without working and be none the worse for it. You eliminate the stress of financial unhappiness and anxiety from your life. Your finances are based on choices rather than urgencies. Instead of putting out fires or living from paycheck to paycheck, you can relax and enjoy your life.

The millionaires in this book consciously created a plan for the kind of lives they wanted to lead, then they worked the plan. Their lives were more meaningful because they had a purpose and made the right choices to match.

When I was a young man I observed that nine out of the ten things I did were failures. Not wanting to be a failure, I did ten times more work.

– Theodore Roosevelt

THE COST OF BOUNCED CHECKS

New figures from Bankrate.com show that there are more than 125 million bounced checks every year. Each one costs consumers from $20 to $35. To avoid that fee, more people are getting overdraft protection, a credit line provided by the bank to prevent bounced checks. Be careful to read the small print, however.

According to BankRate, the credit line could cost you more than the bounced checks! Some banks charge higher interest on lines of credit. At 18% or higher with a fee of $15 to $20 a year, the "protection" may not be worth it. If that's the case, ask your bank to designate a special savings account to your checking account that will automatically transfer funds to cover any overdrafts and save you those added fees.

TRACK YOUR SPENDING WITH DEBIT CARDS

When you are beginning to organize your finances, one of the challenges is keeping track of the money you spend. Cash flow is the culprit that most often interferes with the best laid plans for savings and investments.

I recommend Jean Chatzky's Spending Tracker. It's a good option.

GET A SPENDING TRACKER

One good way to keep track of your money is to use a spending tracker, like the one available on Jean Chatzky's website, www.jeanchatzky.com. You can fill in the money you spend and immediately see what you have left. She promises it can help you live within your means—and enjoy it! Check it out.

Another way of tracking your spending is by using your debit card instead of cash. If your ATM card has a Visa or MasterCard logo on the bottom, it is a debit card. The money is taken directly out of your checking account. Unlike a credit card, your debit card does not incur interest or accumulate unpaid balances. Unlike cash, your debit card will allow you to have a complete record of all your expenditures via your monthly bank statement.

If your account is available online, you can probably check your current statement 24 hours a day. It can then be downloaded into a money management program such as Quicken, QuickBooks, or Money. Follow this plan and you will have saved yourself hours of note-taking and calculations. With your money management program, you can quickly create charts of your expenditures by category. Since the difference between what we *actually* spend and what we *think* we spend is sometimes surprising, this is a terrific way to keep track of your spending.

If you don't go after what you want, you'll never have it.
If you don't ask, the answer is always no.
If you don't step forward, you're always in the same place.

– Nora Roberts

COVERING YOUR ASSETS

Longevity is a drag when you don't have the money to pay for it. Between the latest health discoveries and the regular onslaught of scientific breakthroughs (like mapping the genome), some of us are in danger of living full, healthy lives for a very, very long time!

If you've been basing your retirement income on a life expectancy of 10 or 15 years past retirement, think again. You might need 20 to 35 years of income—or more, if you retire earlier. Your retirement portfolio may last for part of that time, but it is likely to fall woefully short toward the end, if things continue as they are.

BOOK REFERENCE

Barbara Weltman is known as "America's most trusted financial advisor." She is a regular financial advisor on CNBC, CNN, Bloomberg, and *The Today Show.* Now she's put together some of her most valuable advice in a new book called *The Very Shrewd Money Book: Your Personal Action Plan for Greater Wealth.*

Motley Fool suggests one alternative: Live each day as if it were your last. Stop worrying about it and kick back. As soon as the money gives out, move in with your kids! You paid for them when they were young. Now it's their turn!

If that option doesn't appeal to you, you might consider asset allocation. In a recent newsletter, Motley Fool explains that asset allocation involves putting part of your portfolio into three primary markets: cash, stocks, and bonds. Since each one moves at a different rate, you will minimize your risk and increase the likelihood that your assets will continue to grow.

BE A FOOL

The Motley Fool has a financial newsletter dedicated to educating, amusing, and enriching their readers in the area of smart investments. You can become a registered fool for free at www.fool.com/community/registerregister.asp?ref=Yo&source=Yo.

For more valuable tips, see The Motley Fool: Managing Your Retirement—Investing Your Nest Egg Foolishly at www.fool.com/retirement/manageretirement/manageretirement6.htm.

My interest is in the future, because
I'm going to be spending the rest of my life there.

– Charles Kettering

CAN YOU CREATE MULTIPLE GENERATIONS OF WEALTH?

You bet. If I can do it, so can you.

My personal goal is to create four generations of wealth for my family. In my case, I manage an investment account for my parents to help increase the returns they receive, numerous accounts for my wife and myself, and another for my daughter. I have also set up a financial scenario for my future grandchildren. That's four generations. I recommend starting with yourself, then building out as far as you can. I can vouch for the fact that, once you start creating wealth for unborn generations, it's a very good feeling!

One of the primary tools that you can use is a "stretch" IRA, also known as a "multi-generational IRA." First, you'll need to accumulate enough assets so that you will not need much or any income from your retirement plan. And don't take any money out of it until you are required to at age 70½.

At that time, you must start to take the required minimum distribution (RMD), but the balance will continue to grow tax-free. Assuming that your spouse does not need the income, you can make a child or, better yet, a grandchild, the beneficiary. After your death, the beneficiary will receive the funds. They will only be required to take the RMD. The total balance will continue to grow on a tax-deferred basis as the years go by.

If you are able to earn a rate of return greater than the amount paid out for the RMD, the balance will not get depleted, even over the course of one or two lifetimes. That is the ultimate example of letting your money work for you.

EXERCISE: WHAT ARE YOUR GOALS?

No one can choose your goals but you.

Take a moment to think about your future. Then create three columns with these headings: What are your financial needs for this month? This year? The next 10 years?

Write down a list of ideas under each category.

Then ask yourself: What would I like to achieve financially? Fill in your answers under each of the headings above.

Review this list carefully. How can it be refined?

As I've said, a consultation with a financial advisor can be very beneficial to help you learn what's possible for you financially. You may be able to realistically expand your goals much further than you've imagined. This list is a good beginning. Take it with you on your first meeting with your advisor. It will help them help you create the best savings and investment program.

Although it's not a new method, changes in tax law have made this IRA more effective than it was in the past. The challenge is to accumulate enough other assets so that you do not need much income from your retirement plan. It is also important to note that these assets are subject to estate tax, so you may need to carry enough life insurance, under the protection of an irrevocable life insurance trust, to cover the taxes that will be due upon inheritance.

Proper planning for wealth that lives on after you've gone could include two things:

- The accumulation of assets, especially retirement plans, along with other tax-favored vehicles, and
- Proper distribution, such as wills and trusts, and the use of a stretch IRA.

These methods make it very possible to know the comfort of providing for the people you love long after your death.

Numerous websites include information on stretch IRAs. Your own financial advisor can also provide you with further information. Here are a few websites to check out first. A search for "stretch IRA" should bring up their latest articles on the subject.

- www.fool.com
- www.kiplingers.com
- moneycentral.msn.com

Investing is simple, but not easy.

– Warren Buffet

BUILD WEALTH AT WORK: CREATE WEALTH THROUGH YOUR BENEFITS PACKAGE

As part of its retirement savings education campaign entitled "Savings Matters," the Department of Labor partnered with the Consumer Federation of America to develop a series of advertisements to encourage retirement savings. The ads encourage workers aged 50 and older to save more as their retirement nears. Other ads highlight ways young workers can achieve a secure retirement by saving over their working life and participating in plans that offer matching employer contributions.

For details, visit www.dol.gov/ebsa/savingmatters.html#section5. Other great resources on this site offer answers to these questions:

- Do you want an extra $100,000?
- How can you earn 100% return on savings?
- Are you passing up free money?
- Over 50 and want to save some more for your retirement?

BUILDING A LIFE LEGACY

True wealth, of course, involves a lot more than leaving cash to your heirs and loved ones. To build a life legacy, you must include not only financial security but all of the elements we've been discussing in this book. Each of them accrue to the creation of a life you can be satisfied to live.

Dave Ramsey, renowned financial advisor and author of *More than Enough*, offers a few important things you can do to ensure that you have more than enough in your life:[42]

- **Live by your values.**
  Research shows that there is a strong correlation between people with high integrity and comfortable net worth.

- **Have a vision.**
  This vision is the big choice, followed by all the smaller ones that get you there. If you don't choose what you want in your life, you'll drift.

[42] Ramsey, Dave. "Financial Adviser's Keys to Having More than Enough," www.bottomlinesecrets.com (October 2002).

- **Never lose hope.**

  So many people give up too soon. Your goals are often far more accessible than you think.

- **Work hard.**

  Never settle for mediocrity or start taking things for granted. Put passion into everything you do. Give it your best. Not only will your results be better, but you'll enjoy your life more!

- **Have patience.**

  Some of the best things take time. No one likes the waiting. Those who have the most success learn to adapt to it.

- **Look to love for satisfaction.**

  The material things in your life are great. They make life easier and more comfortable. But ultimately, it's your relationships with other people that will bring you the most satisfaction in life.

- **Keep giving.**

  Don't let yourself fall prey to stinginess—with time, money, or emotions.

We make a living by what we get,
but we make a life by what we give.

– Winston Churchill

In the end, the single greatest investment you can make is to invest in yourself. Of all my investments, in every possible area you can think of, my greatest returns have always come from my investments in myself. Take courses, such as my seminar, or others listed in the link on my website, to improve your understanding of your true potential. Most people sell themselves too short and never live to anywhere near their potential. They never experience the joy that could be theirs by accepting the challenge of life-changing, transformational growth. It can be scary, and may seem expensive, but the returns are beyond any riches that you will acquire by any other means.

The more you learn about how to be happy, healthy, and wealthy, the more you will grow as a human being. Your relationships will be stronger, your satisfaction and contentment with life will be greater, and you will be able to command more in financial terms.

When you invest in yourself, you can expect the biggest payoff yet.

Life begets life. Energy becomes energy.
It is by spending oneself that one becomes rich.

– Sarah Bernhardt

One of the most tragic things I know about human nature is that all of us tend to put off living. We are all dreaming of some magical rose garden over the horizon—instead of enjoying the roses that are blooming outside our windows today.

– Dale Carnegie

Conclusion

ARE YOU READY?

Life is either a daring adventure . . . or nothing.

– Helen Keller

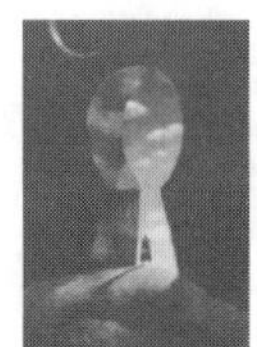

CONCLUSION

Are You Ready?

Now that you know it's possible to completely change your life, only one question remains: Are you ready to do it?

Every single day you make decisions that directly affect your happiness, your health, and your wealth. If you're like most people, you've been taking some of these things for granted. You weren't really convinced that each and every one of them was in your control. Somehow, it was easier and more natural to think that you were at their mercy.

If things didn't go quite right, you weren't very happy. But that seemed like something that happened to you from the outside. No one told you that you were in charge of your own happiness. No one said, "Things won't always go the way you like, but your happiness is always up to you." So you assumed the happiness in your life would come and go, as if it were slipping through your fingers.

Now that you've read this book, you know differently.

Happiness is at your command. Investing in the relationships that matter will amplify your happiness a thousandfold. My own happy, thirty-year marriage is a testament to that.

Refusing to allow negative thoughts to swamp your mind will virtually eliminate your day-to-day malaise. All of the tips, books, references, and suggestions in the Happiness section have emphasized over and over that your happiness is entirely up to you.

And what about health? This is yet another area where you may have felt like a victim. "I just can't lose those 10 pounds" is a common refrain, when changing your eating habits and exercising every day is a well-known cure. Maybe you've felt tired or stiff at the end of the day and you said, "I'm getting too old ..." because you've heard other people get away with that excuse. It's just another way of expressing the feeling that your life is out of your control.

Now you know my story, and if I can get rid of my spare tire and be more fit at 53 than I've ever been in my life, it's not about age at all. It's about learning what to do, then doing it.

The same is true for wealth.

As you've seen in this book, the majority of wealthy people aren't the "lucky" ones. They're the hard workers. They're people who made a choice to be wealthy, who've taken the time to learn how to do it, and who have gone after it with all their heart. Those who are happiest with their wealth have learned that it isn't about the money. It's about creating a secure, comfortable life, filled with options—for themselves and their loved ones—for generations!

You are not the victim, when it comes to happiness, health, or wealth. The reins are in your hands. If you never pick them up, that's nobody's fault but your own. It's up to you to use them.

Many of life's failures are people who did not realize
how close they were to success when they gave up.

– Thomas Edison

YOU'VE GOT THE POWER

No matter what you've been led to believe, you're not at the mercy of your life. You have the power to change in ways that will far exceed your wildest dreams.

As I've said from the beginning, knowledge is all-powerful. Anything you can do to increase your base of knowledge will be rewarding. But knowledge without action is wasted talent. You *must act*—and act with passion—if you're going to accomplish anything worthwhile in your life.

You can't build a reputation on what you are going to do.

– Henry Ford

Take a moment to imagine this. The plans for change you're making right now are *just the start* of what's possible for you. Right now, you're hoping that I'm right. You're hoping this will really work. Until it works, you're not really certain.

I guarantee you, if you make your plan and follow through, it will work. You'll soon know that for yourself. And once you do, you'll have a firsthand experience of what I've been telling you all along: You can achieve whatever you want, if you're willing to do what it takes! Don't let anyone tell you otherwise.

Remember, according to the laws of aerodynamics, bumblebees can't fly. Their body weight is too great for their wingspan. If you built a plane like a bumblebee, it would be impossible for it to fly. It would never get off the ground. The experts say it's impossible for the bumblebee too. But bumblebees don't ask anybody else if they can fly. They just fly anyway.

You're only beginning to discover what's possible for you. Once you succeed in meeting the goals you're setting now, once you recognize your own power, you will see what you can do. And your *next* set of goals will be truly amazing!

Success is a journey, not a destination.

– Unknown

The best way to begin is to learn as much as you can. Check out the websites, books, and other references I've mentioned throughout the book, many of which are linked on my website at www.gethappy-gethealthy-bewealthy.com. Take my seminar and as many other classes as you can. Make yourself an expert on the ways to improve your own life.

Decide what you are going to do to get happy, get healthy, and be wealthy this year. For each area that I've touched on in this book, set your goals and make your plan.

Then put that knowledge to work. Take meaningful action to attain the material sufficiency and self-actualization that comes with living a full, abundant, complete life. Attend my seminar and spend one day creating a plan that will change your life.

Strive to become so successful that your success becomes contagious! The more successful you are, the more you can positively impact the lives of your friends, family, and loved ones. Work to accomplish things that other people don't believe can be done. Those who don't believe such change is possible will be the ones who are most surprised—and inspired—when, like the bumblebee, you just fly anyway.

The tragedy in life doesn't lie in not reaching your goal.
The tragedy lies in having no goal to reach.

– Benjamin Mays

HOW BADLY DO YOU WANT IT?

David Gleicher is recognized as developing the formula for change. He says that change *only* occurs when these three things are greater than your natural human *resistance to change:*

- Dissatisfaction
- Vision
- First steps

The purpose of this book and my seminars is to help you identify the areas of dissatisfaction in your life. I want to help you create a future vision that is so strong, so compelling, and so convincing that you are totally committed to accomplishing it. I want to help you take the first steps in order to start a plan of action that will really work for you. I want to help you overcome that resistance that has held you back previously.

Change = Dissatisfactiom × Vision × First Steps > Resistance

This is what it's going to take for you to change your life!

You have to want it. Bad. You have to be *so dissatisfied* with the way things are now that you have the momentum to push through that resistance without even slowing down. You have to have a *vision* to pull you forward toward your goals. Then, you have to know what your first steps are going to be—and take them.

- How dissatisfied are you right now?
- Do you have a vision of how great your life could be?
- What are the first steps you're going to take?

Now is the time to get started. A year from now, you could be living the life you've always wanted. Why put it off for another day?

If you take too long in deciding what to do
with your life, you'll find you've done it.

– George Bernard Shaw

THE ONE-YEAR PLAN

A one-year plan, with many short-term markers, is what you need to absolutely, positively reach your goals. You can completely change your life in a single year.

At my live seminars you set your plan in place. I will personally follow up with you by e-mail for 52 weeks to help you reach the goals you've set for yourself, and provide new, current information to help keep you motivated.

Having experienced such success myself, I want to prove to you that you can succeed too.

Once you have experienced this kind of success, you will quickly move on to tackle greater challenges until they are fulfilled. Your life will never be the same.

I challenge you to change your life now.

- Are you ready to get healthy—from the inside out?
- Are you ready to get happy—every day?
- Are you ready to be wealthy—beyond your wildest dreams?

It's all about choice. It's up to you to consciously choose. I challenge you to adopt a new mantra, and recite it daily.

Each day I will consciously choose:

- *Irrepressible happiness*
- *Optimal health and mental well-being*
- *Abundant, life-enriching wealth.*

Life is not going to deliver these things to you on a platter. You have to make them happen in your life. No one can do that but you. You have to choose. I challenge you to make that choice now.

Are you ready?

Nobody who ever gave his best regretted it.

– George Halas